Quick & Easy Getaways
Michigan Back Roads

by

Ron Rademacher

Have Fun
Ron

First Edition

Back Roads Publication
P.O. Box 235
St. Helen, Michigan 48656

TABLE OF CONTENTS

Albion Getaway 1

Alcona Getaway 7

Baldwin Getaway 17

Beaver Island Getaway 23

Bellevue Getaway 29

Buchanan Getaway 33

Charlevoix Getaway 39

Clare Getaway 45

Coldwater Getaway 51

Croswell - Lexington Getaway 57

Crystal Lake Getaway 61

Escanaba Getaway 65

Fenton Getaway 71

Grosse Ile Getaway 77

Historic Shiawassee Getaway 81

Huron Jewel Getaway 85

Kalkaska Getaway 89

Les Cheneaux Getaway 93

Lewiston Getaway 99

Manistique Getaway 105

Old Town Getaway 111

Other Great Lakes Getaway 115

Rochester Area Getaway 123

Saline Getaway 131

Tawas Bay Getaway 135

Three Waterfalls Getaway 139

Tip Of The Thumb Getaway 143

Top Of The Lake Getaway 149
Walloon Getaway 153
White Lake Getaway 159

Quick & Easy Getaways Michigan Back Roads

by

Ron Rademacher

Back Roads Publications
P. O. Box 235
St. Helen, Michigan 48656

Acknowledgments

No book is the work of just one person. This one wouldn't have been written without the unwavering support and suggestions of the sponsors.

Cover Photograph – Kitch-Iti-Kipi

Thanks are due to all the folks in the small Michigan towns who have made time for my presentations, endless questions and photographic intrusions.

A special thanks to the people and organizations who supported and sponsored this project.

Quick & Easy Getaways
Michigan Back Roads

by Ron Rademacher

Published by
Back Roads Publications
P. O. Box 235
St. Helen, Michigan 48656

ISBN-13: 978-0-9883138-6-6

ALBION GETAWAY

Whether you arrive in Albion by car, train, paddle in on the Kalamazoo River, or by one of five different trails, every route leads to an historic downtown in the midst of a renaissance. The plans for this transformation are big. The residents have done so much that Albion has been designated a "Project Rising Tide Community". The main thoroughfare has new street-scaping. A new hotel has opened downtown, the Bohm Theatre, circa 1929, has been restored. New shops and a microbrewery have opened. The Ludington Center has also opened downtown. It is another instance of the city and Albion College working together. The facility includes smart classrooms, conference rooms and offices. The first-floor open space that can host anything from class reunions to wedding receptions to school proms.

Albion easily qualifies as a "trail town", there are five trails that converge here. Trail activities include hiking, walking, paddling and biking. The Albion River Trail runs along the south bank of the Kalamazoo River. The trail is a little over a mile and an half long, running from McClure Riverfront Park at the west end, through town, to Victory Park on the east end. It's paved so the trail is open to walking and wheel sports, but no motorized vehicles, except motorized wheelchairs. The Albion River Trail is part of a larger trail system known as Route #1 of the Great Lake to Lake Trail. Route #1 is a 240 mile route from Port Huron to South Haven. Route #1, through Albion, connects 15 different trails into one continuous pathway. The Calhoun County Trail is a 6-mile non-motorized pathway through nature areas from Memorial Bridge all the way through Battle Creek. Finally, one branch of the Iron Belle Trail intersects the other trails. It is the longest designated state trail in the United States and runs from Belle Isle Park in Detroit, to Ironwood in the Upper Peninsula.

There are several other nature areas that add to the beauty of the town. Albion has more parks per capita than anywhere else in the country including, the Equestrian Center, the Whitehouse Nature Center and Reiger Park where the kayak launch is. The area known as the "forks", at the confluence of the north and south branches of the Kalamazoo River, is where local heritage is celebrated every year at the "Festival of the Forks". Victory Park is the "central park" of Albion. The park offers several venues for sports and a trail for hiking and biking. This is where everybody gathers for a series of musical events throughout the summer at the band shell. In the winter months it is sledding and the Cardboard Classic that are the main attractions.

One way to see it all is to take one of the walking tours. There are four different Self-Guided Walking Tours in town. One is the Architectural Tour with a dozen locations. The architectural tour is enhanced by the scavenger hunt. An available brochure depicts several structural details to locate across town. Another is the

Purple Gang Tour and the third is the Riverside Cemetery Tour. In addition to those, there is the River Walk. Art Walk is a self-guided Tour of sculptures, outside murals and the Bobbitt Center for the Visual Arts the campus. Along with the walking tours are several festivals. The Festival of the Forks has been held annually since 1967 on the third full weekend in September. Over 10,000 people attend this celebration. There is the Cruise-In for historic cars July, Sweet Seasons Apple Orchard for cider and donuts in the fall, and Albion Aglow is the annual Christmas celebration. All of this information is available at the Chamber Visitors Center.

Like everything else around here, the history is unique as well. The Gardner House was built around 1875 and serves as museum and headquarters for the Albion Historical Society. The basement has the old tool room, a reminder of a time when projects were done by hand. The house has preserved the 1900-era kitchen, original wallpaper and a Victorian bedroom and bathroom. There is a picture of Julie Calhoun Blakely, the original mother of Mother's Day. The first Mother's Day is believed to have originated in Albion in the late 1800's. Other exhibits rotate through the year including memorabilia of three Albion veterans who were Tuskegee Airmen.

The Bohm Theatre, downtown, has been lovingly restored through the efforts and dedication of local citizens. It is the venue for events all year, including the Blues at the Bohm blues concerts. Another historical aspect of the theatre is that it was purported to be a meeting place for members of the Purple Gang. Two of those infamous gangsters, Sam Bernstein and Louis Fleischer, lived in Albion during Prohibition, where they oversaw the distribution of bootleg liquor to "western" gangs. Albion's location between Chicago and Detroit made it an ideal meeting place. The crooks from Chicago would journey to Albion by rail and stay at the Parker House Inn. On Sunday evenings they would buy tickets at the Bohm, and take seats in the balcony right below the noisy projection booth. The noise helped cover their conversations with the "Purples". Today there is a row of purple seats in the first row of the balcony as a reminder of the Purple Gang and its history with the Bohm Theatre.

Some cemetery's preserve history in a special way. The Riverside Cemetery has been designated an historic site by the Michigan Preservation Office and placed on the State Register of Historic Sites. The cemetery, on the edge of town, is huge at more than 40 acres and has several unusual features. The first burial in this cemetery was in 1837, the same year Michigan became a state. The cemetery helps preserve the ethnic diversity of Albion through the existence of special burial areas. There are areas known as "The Russian Section with those distinctive crosses," "German Hill," and a section for African-American veterans from World War I. A private Catholic cemetery contains the remains of people from Italy, Lithuania, and Poland. In addition to the unique tombstones, the cemetery includes a very impressive mausoleum.

With all there is to see and do, some visitors decide to stay over. Two of the best options are the Albion Heritage B&B and the Palmer House B&B. Both are historic buildings that have been beautifully preserved. The innkeepers at both are excellent cooks and they know all details about history and what is going on around town. The Palmer House was built in the 1800s and has a 19th Century atmosphere with 21st Century amenities. The atmosphere is created by the period antiques throughout the home. The rooms each feature unique antiques.

The Albion Heritage Bed and Breakfast occupies a stately Georgian Revival home, built in 1912. With the finest of amenities; Queen-sized beds, private baths, shower massage jets, towel warmers, cable TV/DVD/VHS/CD, wireless Internet connection, air conditioning, and gourmet breakfasts, this B&B cannot be beat. If you stay at either, be sure to say hello for me, both bed and breakfasts helped sponsor this chapter.

Dining options range from a gourmet coffee house, to a family owned restaurant that has been here for 100 years, to the new Bistro, inside the Courtyard by Marriott. It is all here, downtown, fast food, slow food, craft foods and brews. The newest addition is the Albion Malleable Brewing Company. Named for the Albion Malleable Iron Company, which closed in 2002, it will only start off with a small kitchen, selling the beers it brews, they are already looking towards a future wine license to make ciders.

There is something else rare and wonderful here. Albion is home to the largest Anagama style kiln in North America. Anagama is a Japanese term meaning "cave kiln". Every fall, artists here light the kiln for 10 straight days and fire more than 2,000 pieces of pottery. The kiln, 55 feet by 14 feet, is built of brick and is just one of the remarkable attractions to be found at Albion College. The kiln is heated entirely by wood and uses as much as a face cord every half hour at the kilns most intense heat. Plain sculpted clay goes in and masterpieces of pottery come out to be displayed at the on site gallery.

ALCONA GETAWAY

Some getaways involve nature areas, shopping, history, touring and, almost always, traffic. If you want to get away, for a day, try Alcona County it has all of these, except the traffic. Even at the peak of the tourism season, it is easy to get around Alcona. The only time it gets crazy is during Harmony Week. That is the one time of the year where space can be limited. In addition to Lake Huron, there are several inland lakes for boating, swimming, fishing or a shoreline picnic. You could take a driving tour of Alcona County Historical Sites, you could enjoy a day, or more, exploring the wilderness areas. Some visitors go just to test their skills on the challenging golf courses scattered across the county from Glennie to Greenbush to Spruce. Some go for the starlit heavens visible from the Dark Sky Park.

Most everyone knows that the biggest arts and crafts street fair in Michigan is in Ann Arbor. What many don't know is that the second biggest is Harmony Week in Alcona County. Hundreds of artists and craftsmen come each September to transform the area around the Craftmaker's Cabin into a gigantic art fair. Harmony Week isn't the only festival in the area. Barton City's claim to fame is the "The Biggest 4th In The North." On Independence Day it has been known to have 10,000 people flood the streets to watch the famous parade in the morning and stay for the fabulous fireworks display at dusk. Barton City's population consists of a lot of people who have been born and raised here, and a lot of people from down state, who have been attracted to this area for all it has to offer. These are just two of the celebrations to enjoy in during the year.

History buffs love this place. The Alcona County Historical Society has preserved the past for all to explore. The drive along Lake Huron is part of the Lake Huron Discovery Tour. A short list of historical destinations includes, a one room schoolhouse, train depots, lighthouse, and turn of the century churches. Visitors will find some of these out on the Quilt Block Trail. If you want the guided tour, the historical society provides an excellent booklet describing three different driving tours. Here are just a few historic destinations, in no particular order.

Black River – The Village of Black River was a fishing community.   Eventually, lumbering operations started up and the railroad arrived. By the 1890's, Black River was the second largest community in the Alcona-Lake Huron region. When the trees were gone, the lumbermen left and the rails were pulled up. Black River survives today, unlike the ghost towns of Alcona and Springport, due to that fine harbor. There is a nice waterfront park and locals can be found fishing the river.

Old Stone Church - There is historic architecture in every town and at many crossroads across the Alcona region. In the 1880s the wooden frame First Presbyterian Church of Alcona was built. It was destroyed by fire in 1924, but was rebuilt by volunteers using field stone gathered from the surrounding area. Known today as the Old Stone Church, it is located at 4505 E. Shaw Rd.

Lincoln Depot & Museum – The Lincoln Depot is the last remaining depot of its kind in northeastern Michigan. Local communities were dependent on the railroads and depots during the lumbering era. The first rail service to this area passed through Lincoln from the south and continued north through Ossineke to Alpena. The Lincoln Train Depot was originally called the West Harrisville Depot. It was built in 1886 by the Detroit, Bay City and Alpena Railroad and has been standing since the 1880's. The depot is now a museum and tells the story of the railroads and lumber in this area.

The Craftmaker's Cabin – The Craftmaker's Cabin is just south of the traffic light in downtown Harrisville. The cabin is the result of a WPA project in 1936. It was used to house the Resort and Information Bureau. The cabin is a rustic log building with a massive stone fireplace and a staircase made of flattened logs. The handrail for the staircase is made of a single curved log. This is a favorite stop for those looking for local homemade arts and crafts.

Sturgeon Point – Sturgeon Point is a major destination as it is the location of the Old Bailey School, the Sturgeon Point Lighthouse and the offices of the Alcona County Historical Society. The Bailey School is one of the few hewn log, one-room schoolhouses still standing in Michigan. It was built in 1907 for the children of logging crews. Since it was moved to Sturgeon Point in 1998, it has been nearly completely restored.

The light house was built in 1869 and is still operational. The grounds hold examples of boats, rudders and Lake Huron equipment. The gift shop has plenty of cool items and there is excellent rock and shell hunting along the shore. The keepers house is now a museum and is open Memorial Day - mid September. After you tour the buildings you might want to walk from the Sturgeon Point Lighthouse out to the point itself. Sturgeon Point earned its name because of the fantastic numbers of sturgeon that came in to spawn.

Quilt Block Trail – Another way to tour the historic structures in the Alcona region is the Alcona Quilt Block Trail. This is the original Michigan quilt block trail and covers most of Alcona County. A driving map is available at many businesses and at the Chamber of Commerce office in Harrisville. NOTE: Many roads in this area are not paved.

While touring the historic destinations, be sure to pause and enjoy the natural wonders. This is the Huron National Forest and it is full of wildlife, scenic views and trails. Nature areas beckon from the Black River, to Hubbard Lake, to Jewell Lake, to the Au Sable River. This is a nature lovers paradise in every season. The

Corsair Trails to the south are famous among cross country ski enthusiasts. The Hoist Lake foot travel area encompasses nearly 10,000 wilderness acres. It has 19 miles of trails for hiking and back-country skiing. Then there is little known Negwegon with it's beautiful trails and dark skies.

Hubbard Lake is an 8,800+ acre in northern Alcona County. It is seven miles long and two miles wide so there is plenty of room. The lake averages about 32 feet in depth with a maximum of around 85 feet. The lake is stocked regularly so the fishing is great in the warm months and for ice fishing. Anglers, even the challenged like me, will find bass, yellow perch, northern pike, tiger muskie, trout and walleye. DNR boat launches are available.

The Au Sable Highbanks are found on the world famous Au Sable River. The river runs more than 100 miles, through some of the most beautiful wilderness in lower Michigan, before flowing into into Lake Huron. Far up atop the bluffs along the river the Au Sable Highbanks Trail affords some of the most spectacular scenic views in Northern Michigan. The path to the bluffs isn't very long and it will only take a short time to reach the split rail fence that runs along this section of the Highbanks Trail. The fence runs along an overlook that is more than 100 feet above the river. At the overlook you can simply pause, rest, and take in the breathtaking view of the bend, in the Au Sable River, spread out below. In the winter, you might be the only person taking in the pure air, high up on the bluffs.

We have warm memories of camping and roasted marshmallows when we think of State Parks in Michigan. Negwegon State Park, is one of the wildest parks left, an artesian well is the only source of water. The park is reached by land after driving along a very rough sand trail for several miles. It is actually easier to get to the park by canoe or kayak. No vehicles are allowed inside the park, so you hike to your campsite. There are only four campsites, with rustic facilities, spread along the two mile main trail. Each campsite has its own private beach on Lake Huron.

Between campsite 3 and campsite 4 the trail splits. The branch to the right will take you across a prairie to campsite 4. Exploring the prairie will reveal an old stone water well and the foundations of an old cabin. The story is told that during the last century, a free black man lived here all alone and disappeared without a trace. Hike into this remote place during the winter and you will wonder how anyone could survive in this isolated location, 100 years ago, all alone. If you take the trail to the left before you enter the prairie, you can hike for a couple more miles as the trail loops back toward the parking area.

The Hoist Lake foot travel area encompasses almost 10,000 acres of pine, aspen and hardwood forest. There are 19+ miles of looped trail. Hiking trails and back-country skiing are permitted, however, there are no groomed trails. There are pothole lakes and beaver floodings. Cross country skiing and hiking range from moderate to more difficult. The difficulty is mostly a result of the length of some of the loops. Hunting and fishing are permitted in season.

Alcona Park encompasses 1,100 acres, above the Alcona dam, with three miles of shoreline on each side of the Au Sable. The park is surrounded by the Huron National Forest and is a favorite home away from home for vacationers. The river provides quality fishing of Walleye, Pike, Perch, Bass and Trout. Some people go just for the canoeing, boating, swimming, and wildlife viewing. Over 450 campsites and cabins are available.

You can find even more fun out on the side roads. It is worth the trip to drive over to Curran for one of their festivals. They are, after all, the Black Bear Capital of Michigan. Then there is the Cedar Brook Trout farm. Generations of young people have had their very first fishing experience at Cedar Brook. The trout farm has natural spring ponds where trout are raised for stocking purposes. In the summer months they are open for public fishing. Not only are you certain to catch fish, the service includes free equipment, cleaning, and packaging. This place has been creating memories for more than 75 years.

One place, just across the county line, that shouldn't be missed is the Dinosaur Gardens. This is a park that has a long history and has recently been restored. When you get just a little way into the park, it is easy to imagine that you have been transported back in time. Along the trail you will find depictions of an "iguanadon", a velocirapter, an ongoing struggle in a tar pit, a stegosaurus and many more. If you look closely, there is even a dinosaur fish sculpture in the river, near the bridge. The gardens include about 20 acres. In addition to the enormous sculptures, wildflowers abound, giant ferns grow among the cedar trees. On the ridge there are White Pines, Norway Pines, and Hemlock trees. The Dinosaur Gardens required nearly forty years to create and contains over 25 life-size dinosaurs, from various periods of history.

It isn't all nature and history around Alcona. The shopping is pretty good during an Alcona Getaway as well. There are shops, dining spots, art galleries, golf courses and festivals. There are galleries featuring the work of local artists, old time general stores, a place that features all things moose, and small antique shops and flea markets to be discovered along the way. Some people make it here for the first time for one of the unique festivals that take place. There are traditional events from Barton City to Mikado. The Alcona Arts Retreat is an opportunity to revel in nature's beauty, make new creative friends and find inspiration in workshops with one of several experienced, enthusiastic instructors in visual arts, writing and music. Spend a special weekend along the Lake Huron shoreline, as you sharpen your skills in digital photography, hammered dulcimer, oil painting, songwriting, quilted thread painting, flute, pastel painting, classical strings, writing poetry, folk dance or watercolor painting.

First time visitors, to Alcona County, are sometimes surprised at the variety of dining options. There is gourmet coffee, awesome ice cream, sports bars and a long time favorite, Rosa's Lookout for steaks and delicious Italian. You will find wine tasting, eclectic bistro's and the Corner Brew Haus in the old Meulbecks location. When you stop there, don't miss the historic stein door.

Lodging options range from old fashioned "up north" motels and beach resorts to the luxurious accommodations of the Lake Huron Inn with a private beach. A lot of people bring their lodging with them. The campgrounds and Harrisville State Park make this a prime destination for camping. Facilities range from full service to primitive rustic campgrounds.

There is something rare and wonderful here. Alcona County is home to a Dark Sky Park. Dark Sky Parks are areas that are set aside to preserve our rapidly disappearing dark places. Michigan was the first state in the US to protect its own land for the quality of its dark sky. Alcona pursued the rigorous process laid out by the Dark Sky Association. No development will be allowed that will include lights at night, so generations to come will be able to see shooting stars, the aurora borealis, and space stations flying through space overhead.

It is a good idea to check the Chamber of Commerce website before you go. The Chamber maintains an office in the Harbortown Market Place in Harrisville. That is where you can get information, trail maps and festival information. Alcona County is a northern destination and some businesses are seasonal.

BALDWIN GETAWAY

Development has brought us super highways and destinations found at the exits. Thankfully, some Michigan treasures remain quiet and unsullied with little traffic. Out on Route 37 is a town that generations have visited, and to which even the millennials can't wait to return. A getaway to Baldwin will almost certainly involve, fun on the water; within a few miles of downtown there are 156 lakes and 46 trout streams. In town is ice cream, shopping, and a lot of nearly forgotten history. This whole region is within the Huron-Manistee National Forest with its streams, lakes and trails.

Many come here for access to unspoiled natural beauty. The Pere Marquette river is famous around the world as one of the best, fly only, trout streams on earth. In 1884 J. F. Ellis of the Northville Fish Hatchery, brought a can with 5000 brown trout fry in it to this area. He dumped them into the Pere' Marquette river near Baldwin, and that is how the first German brown trout were introduced to American waters. Trout fishing is so much a part of life here that one of their main festivals is the annual Troutarama. It has been going on since the 1950s.

Another unique natural wonder nearby is the Loda Wildflower Sanctuary. This is the only wildflower sanctuary inside a National Forest. Through more than 70 acres and a hiking trail of about 1 1/2 miles you can discover a sampling of wildflower plants that used to cover much of lower Michigan. In fact, more than 200 plants have been identified; you can find them easily by following the trail map brochures that are provided near the trail head. In addition to the wildflowers there are birds galore. The wildflower sanctuary also has a bird checklist available that shows more than 120 varieties of birds to be found in the different habitats.

The sanctuary includes a small spring-fed lake, a wetland area, a creek and marshy areas. There is an oak forest, pine plantations and the remains of an old farm site. A gorgeous place for a quiet break or a full day. There is a picnic area and there are rustic facilities. There are no shops or services and it is important to note that you will have to drive a gravel road to get there. Use Hwy M-37 south out of Baldwin. Take 5-Mile Road west to the intersection with Felch Ave. Turn north on Felch.

Other great reasons to visit Baldwin are the festivals and the unusual shops. Since 1972 the return of spring is celebrated with the Blessing of the Bikes. The "Blessing" started with 4 bikes and 8 riders who gathered at St. Ann Catholic Church to receive a blessing for a safe and happy riding season. From that tiny beginning the festival has grown into a major event. Thousands of motorcycle enthusiasts gather in Lake County in downtown Baldwin, Michigan. The event has grown so popular that it isn't unusual for bikes to be lined up for miles to enter the blessing area, sometimes with less than half an hour before the blessing begins. The entire community joins in the fun to welcome the bikes and the long awaited arrival of warm weather.

In late summer it is Troutarama. For more than seven decades they have been celebrating the rivers and those wonderful trout that populate them. The celebration has grown and now includes a children's fishing derby, carnival, concerts and a grand parade. Whether you go for a day or the whole weekend, there is fun for everyone and superb trout fishing.

No matter why you are in town, there are some must visit businesses here. Perhaps the most famous is Jones Homemade Ice Cream. They have been manufacturing delicious ice cream, using the best quality ingredients, since 1942. When you enter, you will step back in time with oldies music, walls of historical local history and a friendly courteous staff. They are serving thick and creamy malts & shakes, old fashioned sodas, sundaes topped with your favorite topping, whipped cream & nuts. For the specialty shopper there are fruit yogurt smoothies, thick & chunky flurries, and as assortment of no sugar added and fat free products. Souvenirs are available like historical books, maps, postcards and souvenirs.

Pandora's Box, Baldwin, is a specialty shop featuring apparel, gifts, jewelry and footwear for men and women. This shop is where you find those special items that are so hard to find. They have bear mug, up north mugs,

Michigan gifts, cards and books and those great "best of Michigan" decorating items for the lodge or cabin. Down the road a few miles is the old town of Bitely is the Up North Gift Company, he originator of the University of Bitely items. Located within the vast Manistee National Forest area of Michigan, the store has wide selection of gifts, candles, cabin/home decor, candy, gourmet food goodies, jewelry, custom signs, and apparel.

A BIT OF HISTORY

The Lake County Historical Society preserves the long history and local heritage of the region. The original museum buildings were two US Forest Service ranger residences were constructed in 1938 by the CCC/WPA. In 2012 the County of Lake transferred a prime downtown piece of property to the Society for its use. In addition, the Forest Service donated the two ranger residence houses to the Society so the buildings, and their unique history, would be preserved. Since then the buildings and exhibits have been expanded. The property is located at the head of the Rails to Trails bicycle and snowmobile trail so all visitors find it convenient.

Idlewild is a small community just east of Baldwin. It was also known as the "Black Eden". From 1912 through the mid-1960s, Idlewild was an active year-round community and was visited by well-known black entertainers and professionals from throughout the country. At its peak it was the most popular African

American resort in the Midwest and as many as 25,000 would come to Idlewild in the height of the summer season. When the 1964 Civil Rights Act opened up other resorts to African-Americans, Idlewild's boomtown period subsided but the community continues to be an important as a heritage landmark.

Idlewild was the place to perform for musicians and other entertainers who had already "arrived" and for those that were hoping to get noticed. Although the Paradise Club and other nightclubs are now gone, Idlewild holds many fond memories for those who once visited there. The Idlewild Music Fest celebrates this musical heritage. The festival brings an unmistakable beat back, to echo across Idlewild Lake and Williams Island, if just for awhile.

There is something rare and wonderful here. The Shrine of the Pines Museum houses the largest collection of rustic white pine furniture in the world. It is the work of one remarkable man. The contents of this Michigan treasure are the life work of Raymond W. Overholzer, more than 200 pieces are on display. The exhibit includes a table made from a 700 lb. stump, a rocking chair of roots so well balanced that one push will set it to rocking 50+ times, a fireplace made of 70 tons of stone, a gun rack with 39 wooden ball bearings and much more. The Shrine of the Pines sits on the Pere Marquette river, a perfect setting for this timeless display from another era.

SOME

ROAD

NAMES

ON

BEAVER ISLAND

ARE

IN

GAELIC

BEAVER ISLAND GETAWAY

Beaver Island, America's Emerald Isle, is full of history and mystery. The interior protects some of the most pristine natural wilderness anywhere in Michigan. Less developed than some other islands, the Beaver Island Archipelago is remote, and rustic' without being primitive. Its' trails, scenic drives, gorgeous bays and abundant wildlife make it a cherished destination for nature lovers, and those seeking a quiet getaway with a slower pace. Though the island is the most remote inhabited island in the Great Lakes, Island Airways can get you there, from the Charlevoix airport, in about 20 minutes. Once on the ground, it is decision time. Head into town, St. James, and check out the shops, museums, and beach? Grab a bicycle and take a tour of some of the unique destinations in the interior of the island like, Protar's Tomb, the Champion Birch tree, and the Beaver Island Head Lighthouse on the southern end of the island? Maybe walk the trail at Barney's Lake, visit the serene beauty of Little Sand Bay, or hike the entire Beaver Island Birding Trail? These are just some of the choices.

Another option is to tour the whole archipelago by water. The Beaver Island Water Trail circumnavigates the entire island. Paradise Bay is suitable for any skill level with kayak or canoe. The rest of the trail can be more challenging. Further out, not recommended for paddling, are Garden Island, High Island, Hog Island, and several smaller islands in Lake Michigan, all uninhabited on a permanent basis. Then there is the abandoned lighthouse out on Squaw Island. An excursion with a qualified captian is the safest way to visit those destinations. A water excursion can include a tour of some of the dozens of ship wrecks dotting the lake bottom. You don't need any special knowledge to explore by water, Archipelago Charters can handle all the details and provide expert local knowledge.

What ever you decide to do on your day trip to Beaver Island, you will notice a different life-style. The pace is much slower than the sometimes frantic pace, 40 miles away on the mainland. The artisans and merchants are happy to see you. They will take time to talk about the history of the island, and the many treasures hidden there. If you plan to explore freelance, a stop at the Community Center for maps, directions and WiFi is a must. The map they have will come in handy when you encounter road signs in Gaelic.

The Community Center is in St. James, in fact, almost everything is. This is the town stretched along the lake shore on Paradise Bay. If you forgot to bring something or just need supplies, the shops and markets should have it. St. James is where the museums are found, except Protar's house and tomb. This is also where you can get out on the water, enjoy the beach and access the extensive trail system that makes 'boodlin' here so much fun.

The roads along the shore, and within the interior of the island, are often unpaved. Those conditions encourage many visitors to bring their bicycles and tour the island that way. For those driving all of the Natural Beauty Roads in Michigan, be sure to travel the stretch from Pogenog Road to Lighthouse Drive. There are great spots to stop all along the way. Protar's tomb is right beside an old logging trail turned road. The Champion Birch Tree is a favorite for picture taking, as is the huge rock known as "The Plug".

Some people travel to Beaver Island just for the Music Festival. For centuries, strains of music have risen from the deep green forests of Beaver Island. There were the drums and chants of Native tribes. The old, forgotten songs of French-Canadian voyageurs, Mormon hymns, and the ballads of the. Music has always been part of life here and the traditional songs celebrate island history. This tradition is continued at the Beaver Island Music Festival. They gather at a place nestled in the upland hardwoods on the west side of the island. As soon as you enter the clearing where the music soars, you are transported to sense of renewal.

The Beaver Island Bike Festival is your chance to experience the unique unspoiled beauty of the island in a fun festival atmosphere. Bikers will ride at their own pace and enjoy incredible scenery, island monuments, historic sites, a beach picnic lunch, a B-B-Q after party, and all that friendly Beaver Islands hospitality. The bike festival is in June welcome the arrival of summer.

The islanders are passionate about their history, and are diligent in its preservation. Beaver Island has been home to many peoples and nations, including a unique American religious monarchy. James Jesse Strang founded a faction of the Church Latter Day Saints. He brought his followers to Beaver Island and reigned for six years as the crowned "king" of an ecclesiastical monarchy. The history of the 'Strangites' can be seen in exhibits at the Print Shop museum, in town. Native Americans have been here for hundreds of years. Eastern Europeans came and settled. The Irish have made the most lasting changes to the island. Some of the roads still bear Gaelic names.

There is a lot to do here so, some visitors decide to stay over. Choices range from water front rooms at the motel, to B&B's to the popular Teeny Motel. Finding good food is no problem either. Choose from a very excellent deli, to fine dining, to a choice of Irish pubs.

There is something else rare and wonderful here. On the west side of the island, below Angeline's Bluff, is an enigmatic circle of stones. Long forgotten, the circle was rediscovered in the 1980s. The construction consists of a circle of glacial boulders that is nearly 400' feet across. The center stone has a hole apparently bored or carved into the center. It takes a bit of tramping around in the forest to get an idea of how big this is. Several of these stones have markings that have been interpreted as an ancient script or rock faces. Another face rock is in front of the museum downtown. The circle of stones is an ancient construction. A large sign, with a map, has been erected at the circle to commemorate the vision and determination of M. T. Bussey, the archaeologist who first recognized the circle as a man-made structure. Her remarkable research continues to determine the age and origin of this site, and the complex of other circles, that are deep in the wilderness of the island.

SAND HILL

CRANES

GATHER

NEAR

BELLEVUE

IN THE

THOUSANDS

EVERY

OCTOBER

BELLEVUE GETAWAY

Bellevue is in south central Michigan, between Lansing and Battle Creek. A quick and easy getaway to Bellevue often involves one of three events that happen there every year. A favorite cabin fever reliever in the spring time, is the opening of the Bellevue Drive In. The opening is as reliable a sign of spring, as the arrival of the robins. The huge outdoor menu is all clean and updated. The car hops are on the job to bring you delicious coney dogs, frosted mugs of root beer, and those mouth-watering onion rings. They still have the best onion rings anywhere in Michigan. I think part of the secret is that they don't even slice the onion until an order is placed.

In the autumn of the year, the second weekend in October to be precise, the Sandhill Crane Festival takes place. The Sandhill Cranes gather by the thousands. This is the second largest gathering of sand hill cranes in the United States. One estimate puts the number between 4,000 and 5,000 cranes. They come flying and soaring in to the wetlands in the Baker Sanctuary, the air filled with that distinctive, almost prehistoric sounding cry. For more than 20 years, the Michigan Audubon Society and the Kiwanis Club have opened the Kiwanis Youth Area to the public, for the festival.

The area where the festival is held is rather wild. The road in, and parking areas, are not paved. The festival is spread around a central building where educational programs and materials are available. There are usually arts and crafts that are on theme, with some very talented sculptors, and other artists on hand. There is an interactive program featuring live raptors. These birds of prey are shown on the hillside by local experts. There are guided walks along the nature trails with expert naturalists, programs about birding and lots of nature exhibits.

In between those two events is a tour by the Historical Society. The tour includes visits to the historical sites around town. Across from the Bellevue Drive In is the Reynolds one room school house, from 1885. Just down the road is the old Lime Kiln and across from that is the Keehne Environmental Area. Standing on the boardwalk there, the ruins of the old lime processing plant are visible. Limestone quarried and processed here was used in the construction of the capitol building in Lansing.

Bellevue has wonderful architecture. The historic old mill, down on the river, is a favorite stop on the historical society tour. The mill has been restored to its original glory. The turbines in the basement still generate electricity by harnessing the power of the river. More information is available at the Historical Museum, across from the Village Hall, which is known for its' completely unique stonework. Then there are those Mastodon Bones. A few years ago a couple fellows were digging on a local farm and discovered a mastodon skeleton. While the village completes a planned Mastodon Museum, the bones are on display at the Bellevue Mini Mall. All are welcome to view the bones from 10,000 years ago. The mastodon exhibit is hands on, so the kids can even touch a couple of them.

There is something else rare and wonderful here. One building downtown has a bit of history and symbolism within the structural stonework. Village Hall sits on the northwest corner of the intersection with the flashing light. It is a two story structure that is unique for the exterior stonework. There is plenty of parking downtown, so it is convenient to walk around this building and study the handiwork of the artisan who carved these stones. As you take in the details, you will realize that these were not simply cut and mortared in. There is a group of stones cut into circles, there is a diamond and even a large arrowhead. The arrowhead on the south wall is about three feet long.

This field stone is the work of Charles H. Secore. The building was completed in the early 1900's and was originally a bank. It turns out that these stones tell a bit of the history of the region. It is said that the circular stones represent the medicine wheels of the Ojibway and Chippewa tribes who inhabited the area. The diamond is the symbol used to represent the four directions by the Ojibway, and the arrowhead is a Chippewa reference, since they were known for making arrowheads. There are more intricately carved stones, including one in the shape of a heart. The entire exterior is a work of art.

BEAR

CAVE

IS

THE

ONLY

CAVERN

IN

THE

LOWER

PENINSULA

BUCHANAN GETAWAY

Buchanan is the only city in Berrien County. Less than 20 miles north of South Bend, Indiana and about 12 miles from Warren Dunes State Park on Lake Michigan, Buchanan is right in the heart of Michigan vineyard country. Here visitors will find the old, they have two distinct historical districts, the new, and natural beauty all around. The St. Joseph River flows here with easy access from the boat launch located off of Red Bud Trail. McCoy Creek, instrumental in the development of the mills in the early days, also runs through downtown. Buchanan keeps growing. The principle shopping district includes antique stores, gift shops and restaurants. Recent development has seen the opening of a taproom by Lehman's Farmhouse with craft beer, wines and cider. Another recent development is Flat Water Farms. They have 100 acres dedicated to growing growing organic hops and other vegetables. They are opening an organic brewery and tasting room. The building that was City Hall is now the Outsmart Escape Room. Inside you engage in an interactive game of spying and escape. Realism is added to the experience by the presence of several old jail cells.

History and the arts play an important part in life downtown. Here you will find the "Tin Shop Theatre" where locals take part in and direct plays. "Pears Mill" is where visitors can see how ground flour was milled and see the waterwheel in action. "The Common" is the spot for entertainment. The Art Center is close at hand for art exhibits and information about festivals. The July 4th celebration here is the biggest in southwest Michigan. As many as 50,000 people have attended in the past. In the winter, they take advantage of the changes in elevation around here. The big event is the "Thrill On The Hill" with all kinds of downhill sledding and racing. The plunge down the 600 foot hill is sure to bring an adrenaline rush.

Nature areas and trails surround the town. Dramatic improvements have been made to the McCoy Creek Trail, a favorite for running, biking or walking. At one time there were 13 mills along the creek that were the foundation of the local economy. Now the trail is up to 5 ½ miles of dog friendly trail through downtown, Spafford Woods and Clark Woods. There is a Buck Sculpture downtown next to the Library. Just follow the "buck prints" in the pavement to the woods where the trail begins. At the intersection of Smith and Oak streets is the McCoy Creek Trail Mural. It shows a map of the creek and the trail with several panels of information and images of historical Buchanan and McCoy Creek. The part of the trail that goes through E. B. Clark Woods gives access to an area of the creek that few could get to. Now there are several spots where scenic views of the ravine and the creek seventy feet below are available. Some say that, in addition to the wildflowers, morel mushrooms can be found along the trail.

Bear Cave is open for tours in the warm months. It is on the St. Joseph River a few miles north of town. The cave was formed over 10,000 years ago as a result of the glacial drift and is the only cavern in Michigan. The glacier receding left behind Tufa and boulders which make up the construction of the cave. This is a small natural cave with multiple rooms. The whole thing is only a couple hundred feet long. There are many details and unusual formations throughout the caverns. There are fossils embedded in the ceiling and walls, glacial boulders, and Cave Pearls. As you descend down the winding stairs into the cavern, you will see a Kansas Boulder thought to be tens of thousands of years old. The passage is about six to eight feet wide, damp, and more than ten feet high. The Tufa deposits that make up the cave walls are about 18 feet thick. While damp, the way is well lit and the various formations are well marked to add to the experience. Toward the back of the cave is a secondary passage that leads to a room with a low ceiling and a large clear pool of water. Beyond the low ceiling and pool is another hidden room. This room is known as the "Slave Room" because it was used to hide slaves making their way to freedom on the "underground railroad". This room also is home to the largest population of Eastern Pipistrelle Bats in lower Michigan. It doesn't happen often, but you might see a bat during your walk through the cave. The exit near the river takes you onto a boardwalk at a small waterfall. The cave was used by bank robbers. The story is told that bandits robbed a bank in Ohio back in 1895. They made their way across the state line and hid out in the cave. That incident led to the cave being used to film the movie "Great Train Robbery" in 1903.

Fernwood Botanic Garden is a favorite destination on Mother's Day. The gardens are in bloom and the woodland trails are awash in wild flowers. Even if the weather is bad, there are the indoor gardens, music and food during this special event.

A few miles west is Warren Woods, the forest primeval. Walking trails wind through the only remaining old growth, climax beech-maple forest in lower Michigan. The gigantic beech and maple trees that form the forest occupy 200 acres, sheltering one of the most beautiful walking trails in southwest Michigan. There are two ways to enter the forest, a small trail head north and the state park entrance south. Regardless of which you choose, there are about 3.5 miles of trails that loop along the Galien River. Near the center of the forest, a fine pedestrian bridge crosses the river connecting the two halves of the woods. The north approach to the bridge descends to the river. On the south side of the bridge, is an interpretive station with information and benches. There are 40 easy shallow steps, down the stairs to the bridge.

There is something rare and wonderful here, the little known Trillium Ravine. This trillium wonderland is just a few miles from Buchanan; it is easily accessible and is home to a couple of rare wild flowers. The area is a mixed beech-maple woodland; and even though it is now nearly surrounded by a housing development, it is home to two species of toad trilliums at the northern limit of their range, the prairie trillium and a species of wood poppy that only occurs in Michigan's southwestern counties. Less than a mile from the busy Interstate 31, the 14+ acre ravine site is nestled between housing developments that have grown up. As you wind around the roads, you will finally see a small sign announcing the ravine as provided by the Michigan Nature Association.

When you enter the forest, it is very open making for an easy walk. There are sugar maples, basswood, ironwood and red oak as well as mature beech trees. By about the first of May, the ground is a riot of wild flowers so thick you can hardly avoid stepping on them. Just a few yards from the road you will find the ravine itself. The walls are simply covered with trilliums as well as, May apples, trout lily and tons of blue violets. There are narrow pathways so you can wander around without trampling the flowers. This is a wild place and the sides of the ravine can be slippery. There is no formal parking lot. Trilliums only bloom for a short time so the trip needs to be late April to mid May. The ravine is on Geyer Road near the intersection of U.S. 12 & 31.

A BIT OF OBSCURE HISTORY

Back in the 1800s a prominent citizen, Joseph Coveney, caused a bit of an uproar when he erected a monument in the city cemetery. The monument was to become his grave marker. The uproar was caused by what he inscribed on the sides of the stone. Mr. Coveney was an atheist and one local newspaper described the inscriptions as "slanderous... against Christianity." One story has it that no local stone carvers would work on the monument so Mr. Coveney had the inscriptions done in England. Once the stone was installed in the cemetery it was discovered, to the horror of the locals, that there was no legal way to have it removed. Mr. Coveney enjoyed the ruckus he caused until his death nearly 20 years later. One article after his death stated that the monument cost $3,000 and was inscribed with "some of the most sacrilegious statements ever uttered by mankind." The monument is in Oak Ridge Cemetery and is visited by atheists to this day.

CHARLEVOIX GETAWAY

They call it "Charlevoix The Beautiful" with good reason. Downtown is impressive year round with a wide variety of shops, galleries, and eateries. The views of the lakes alone is worth the trip. People enjoy boat watching as they pass right through town between Round Lake and Lake Michigan. Some people come here for the arts community, and the festivals that seem to be happening almost every weekend. Others come for the history. This is Hemingway country and the home of those remarkable Earl Young Mushroom Houses. Then there is the natural beauty that is all around. There are more than 20 different trails and nature areas. The beaches and shoreline on Lake Michigan are prime locations for hunting Petoskey stones, while waiting for another incredible sunset. Whatever the reason that brings visitors here, nearly everyone agrees that Charlevoix is, in fact, beautiful.

It takes a little time to explore downtown Charlevoix. It isn't that the downtown district is huge or spread out. It is only a few blocks long, but those few blocks are packed with shops and businesses offering a variety of goodies. You can get your candy fix in a number of shops including Northern Michigan fudge. The art galleries will not disappoint and the choices for fashion can make for a full day of shopping. Elements Gallery is a standout even in Charlevoix. They have been nominated for a Niche Top Retailer award. The shop is just a block from the drawbridge and is filled with unique items, personal accessories, and gifts handcrafted by over 200 American and Canadian artists. This gallery is a standout destination in a downtown district that is famous for unique shops. Excellent quality products combined with professional service, make for an enjoyable experience whether you are buying or just browsing. If you are interested in taking the tour of the Mushroom Houses, a guided tour can be scheduled inside Elements.

The unique architecture of Earl Young Mushroom Houses catches the eye almost immediately. There are nearly 30 of these amazing houses with those distinctive roofs and unusual stone work. Young began in 1919 and continued building for almost 50 years. He used locally available materials like field stone, limestone and cedar-shakes to create those wavy roofs. Each of these houses is different and each was designed to blend in with its surrounding landscape. One house, the Half House, is called that because it looks like it is cut in half. Another has two chimneys that look like melting cement. One has a roof like a mushroom and another has one side that looks like an owl. These details are part of what makes the tour so much fun. The houses have come to be known as Hobbit Houses and Mushroom Houses. The fireplace at the Weathervane restaurant is another example of the awesome stonework in these structures. In addition to Stafford's, there is every imaginable lodging option close to downtown.

When you need a break, downtown has any number of pubs and restaurants. Food choices range from fine dining all the way to really good affordable dining, like those whitefish and chips dinners at the Villager Pub. There are so many delicious dining options, that Charlevoix has an annual Restaurant Week. Each participating restaurant creates a special menu just for that week. The visitors center has all the details so you can plan a "culinary journey" through Charlevoix. If you are going to spend time on the beaches, trails and waterways, you may want to enjoy a picnic. Locals and savvy visitors know that one of the best places for delicious food is Andy's Deli and Party Store. Fresh baked bread and tasty fixings make for mouthwatering subs. Andy's isn't downtown. It is hidden away in a neighborhood on Garfield.

Charlevoix, and the surrounding region have a unique history. This is Hemingway country and is the setting of the Nick Adams stories. Horton's Creek is just a few miles out of town along the Boyne-Charlevoix road. The historical museum has his first marriage license on display along with many other artifacts from the region. Then there is the historic Ironton Ferry. The ride is only a few minutes across the South Arm of Lake Charlevoix; the ferry holds just four vehicles at a time. If you happen to have your cow or sheep with you, the rates for those are still posted at the ferry dock.

While Charlevoix is justly famous for that fabulous

downtown, the nature areas and trails add to the beauty of the whole area. The nature areas are close to town and offer a wide range of opportunities for hiking, skiing and biking. There are nearly two dozen trails and nature preserves to explore. Even during the peak tourism season, there is quiet and solitude close by. South of town is Fisherman's Island State Park with 2,678 acres of fun and five miles of the Lake Michigan shoreline. It isn't actually an island anymore, lower lake levels have turned the island into a peninsula. In the other direction is Young's State Park with the visitor created "inverted forest". Near to town are the Depot Heritage Garden, the Meditation Garden and the Butterfly Garden. The Northpoint Nature Preserve is part of the Sunset Coast Birding Trail. Mount McSauba may be the best kept secret in the area. It boasts a hockey rink, ski mountain and a trail system that is simply gorgeous in the winter. Walk out through the dunes and you will find yourself on a secluded Lake Michigan beach. Another way to explore is a Jordan River float trip. JVOutfitters, just south of town, even offers guided winter rafting on the Jordan River. The ride is unbelievably beautiful. Beaver Island, the most remote on the Great Lakes, is just a short trip away. The island has some of the most unique history of any place in Michigan and is a must visit for bird watchers.

There is something else rare and wonderful here. Just outside of town between Charlevoix and Horton's Bay is the historic Greensky Hill Mission. This is where Peter

Greensky established what became the Greensky Hill Indian United Methodist Church. The church is still there and there is a large Native American cemetery. The real treasure is the council circle. Several tribes would meet at this spot for councils. When you are driving away from the church building, you will come to a sharp curve. If you stop there you will see a house in the distance. Look to the right and you will see a circle of huge old maple trees planted in a circle. Their limbs and branches have a distinctive twisted or bent appearance that indicates that this was a council circle. At one time there were eight trees in the circle, but one has fallen. The circle of trees is on private property. The road to Greensky is gravel. The church is listed in the National Register of Historic Places.

CLARE

MICHIGAN

IS

KNOWN

AS

THE

CITY

OF

FESTIVALS

CLARE GETAWAY

Clare, and Clare County, have always been known in Michigan, as the place where "up north" begins. The county is known at the "Gateway To The North". The town is known as the "City of Festivals". If planning a quick and easy getaway around a festival, Clare is an excellent choice of destination. Something seems to be going on nearly every month of the year. The town turns green for the annual 4-day Irish Festival in March, one of the best known and well-loved events in town. Then, diverse festivals go on all year including, the unique Amish Quilt Auction, Craft Show, and Flea Market the third weekend in May and the Friday and Saturday of the Labor Day holiday.

These and other events often take place in downtown Clare. Downtown has retained its hometown charm with historic architecture, unusual shops and plenty of parking. A getaway could be a relaxing day shopping at The Herrick House or treating yourself at the rightly famous, Cops & Donuts. The downtown shopping district is comprised of several blocks of shops and dining options. This is where you will find cafes like the Herrick House, brew pubs, and dining spots that have been there for 100 years.

Since this is the "Gateway To The North", nature lovers are going to find plenty to their liking. Clare grew up along the Flint & Pere Marquette Railway. That railway bed is now a multi-use scenic trail as part of the Rails to Trails program. There is even camping available with a few blocks of downtown, in Pettit Park, on the Tobacco River. Budd Lake, in Harrison, is famous for fishing and winter sports. Just outside of Clare, is a major destination for sportsmen on a getaway, Jay's Sporting Goods, with its' 70,000+ square feet of the stuff you need for fun outdoors.

The Pere-Marquette Rail Trail is a 30-mile paved trail from downtown Clare to Midland. Soon hikers, bikers, and skaters, will be able to enjoy the extensions to the trail including a section from just west of Clare through Evart, and there are plans to pave more of this trail through Reed City and beyond. This route has been designated as US Route 20, which extends west to the Pacific Coast! No motor vehicles are allowed.

The Harrison campus of Mid Michigan Community College contains a trail system that is open to the public. Open year-round, they are perfect for walking, running, biking, snow shoeing, and cross country skiing. Also in Harrison, the Township has built a wooden platform on the trail, at Budd Lake, to give visitors a nice area to pause and watch the birds and other wildlife in the small pond below.

Between these two is the Snow Snake. Fun for all seasons including, golf, terrain park, tubing, zip lines, an off-road park, and skiing in winter.

Lovers of history and the arts can have a full day getaway discovering the treasures hidden around town. The old railroad Depot as been refurbished and the Mast Murals can be seen at what is now the middle school. The Mast Murals are some of the largest WPA murals in existence, composed by a single artist. These murals were part of the Works Project Administration art project. Each of the four panels is approximately 20-feet high and 8-feet wide. They were painted at the Detroit Institute of Arts, wrapped around stovepipe, and transported by flatbed truck the 170 miles to Clare. The murals illustrate agriculture, peacetime activities, science & education and the emerging gas & oil industry. Along with the Mast Murals, there is also another piece of WPA art on the school grounds, an 8-foot high statue called "*Pioneer Mother*" by Samual Cashwan.

History comes alive through a self-guided land mark tour. Jonesville – Jonesville Rd. half mile north of Muskegon Rd. Known for the railroad bridge, this site was a railway roll-off for timber into the Muskegon River. Meredith – M-18 in Franklin Township, this site became a town in the 1880's due to the intersecting railways. Surrey House – 125 E. Beech, Harrison - Originally named the 'Ohio Tavern" in 1879. Spike Horn Ruins – Corner of E. M-61 & Bus 27, Harrison "Spikehorn" Meyers, renowned for bringing live bears to Michigan's capital when lobbying the State Senate, raised bears at this site. This was a regular stop for those heading "up north" on Old 27.

Campbell City – 101 S. Main St., Temple. Currently named Temple this was an early logging area.

Gerrish Railroad – Roadside Park on US-127 south of Mannsiding Rd. between Clare and Harrison. Named for Scott Gerrish, this site commemorates the first successful railroad in Michigan.

Cornwell Ranch – Cornwell Ave. half mile south of Mannsiding Ave. in Arthur Township, this ranch had a major influence on the development of surrounding communities.

Depression Era Art – Doherty Hotel, Clare Painted by Jay McHugh in 1932.

Works Progress Administration (WPA) Art – Clare Post Office and Clare Middle School - These murals, commissioned following the Great Depression, are federally protected works of art.

Dover Schoolhouse and Ott Log Cabin - Dover & Eberhart Rd. Just south of Dover Rd. and originally named Crawford Settlement, the village of Dover was one of the first settlements in the area. It is now the home of the Clare County Historical Museum, (open Saturday afternoons during the summer).

Farwell Historical Society & Museum – 221 Main, Farwell - Sam Farwell was a man instrumental to railroad development in the area and was director of the Flint and Pere Marquette Railroad.

Wilson State Park – On the shores of Budd Lake in Harrison, the parks main building was constructed by the Civilian Conservation Corp. in 1939 along with a stone residence built using rock from Clare, Missaukee, and

Gladwin counties. Brochures are available around town.

There is something else rare and wonderful here. At the main intersection downtown, sits the Doherty Hotel. Inside is a pub where there is a depression-era work of art. On the wall is a mural, that covers approximately 70 feet. The painting depicts leprechauns making beer, though I would have thought it would be a dark stout. The painting is known as the leprechaun mural. The story goes that, during the depression, an unknown artist made a deal with the owner, or hotel manager, to create a painting in the hotel bar, in return for lodgings.

With all of this to enjoy, many on a day trip decide to stay over. Lodging options range from old time motels, a historic hotel and vintage cabins on the many lakes. Full information about lodging can be found at the Visitors Bureau.

COLDWATER

IS

THE

HOME

OF

THE

LITTLE

RIVER

RAILROAD

COLDWATER GETAWAY

Coldwater is full of surprises. In addition to the excellent shops and galleries, this town has some of the finest turn of the century architecture to be found anywhere in Michigan. There are enough unique things to see and do here, that you could take a number of quick getaways to Coldwater. There is the railroad, that architecture, the opera house, the alligators, antiques and drive in movies. Chicago Avenue, the Great Sauk Trail, is the main thoroughfare. On, and around that picturesque avenue, are distinctive attractions, over a hundred fresh water lakes, and nature areas.

There are two principle shopping destinations in Coldwater Country. Downtown Coldwater has a collection of shops and dining options that will keep visitors plenty busy. From jewelry, to notions to crystals to gourmet coffee, you can find it downtown. Then there are the nearby antique malls that have enough variety that you may need to stay over. Items available there include antiques, furniture, collectibles, clocks, and primitives. New items arrive almost daily. These shops offer true antiques and vintage items at great prices, seven days a week.

One very different attraction in Coldwater is the availability of train rides on the Little River Railroad. Nothing says "the good old days" like the romance of exploring by railroad. Imagine the historic depot, the steam whistle, a coal fired engine, and the call of the conductor, "All Aboard". You would find a window seat, and soon, the sound of the metal wheels clicking along the track signal that you're on your way. While long distance journeys by steam train are a thing of the past, the authentic experience is available by short trips in Coldwater. The company offers round trip excursions to the Sauk River and Quincy. There are several events including a fall color tour run.

The Little River Railroad operates round trip rides of under 2 hours on an authentic 100 year old steam engine train. One locomotive is a 110 steam engine weighing in at about 58 tons. This one of a kind engine is the smallest of its kind ever built for standard gauge rails. Another engine is the Number 1, a 0-4-0T tank steam engine. It still a mystery as to when it was built. Records show that the frame and wheels were built in 1908.

If the train were not enough to make Coldwater a standout, consider the entertainment from an old time drive in to a world class opera house. The Capri Drive In offers a chance to experience an authentic all American drive in. There are few of these left for the youth of today enjoy the way we did. This one is even better with digital video & audio, audio is piped in through car radio on an FM station and a snack bar so cool it was featured on the Food Network's Top 5.

At the other end of the spectrum is the Tibbit's Opera

House. The Tibbits Opera House, on South Hanchett, was built in 1882 and featured 1,000 seats and more than 300 gaslights. By the late 1800s the operator fell on hard times and the Opera House became home to a shooting gallery, bowling alley, billiard parlor and saloon. Eventually, the structure was to be demolished. In 1959, the Tibbits Opera Foundation came to the rescue. World class performances are here once again. Today it comfortably seats about 500 people, with an almost perfect acoustic experience. Tibbits Art Gallery gives local and regional artists of all mediums a place to display their works.

When arriving in downtown Coldwater for the first time, the attention is drawn to the amazing architecture that seems to be on every corner. To tour all of the historic structures preserved here, it is a good idea to get a copy of the Walking Tour from the visitors center. Here is a very small sample of what can be found during the tour.

The Victorian Mansion Inn, on Division Street, was built in 1870. The style is Italianate. The walls are 14 inches thick and each floor has an identical floor plan.

The Clark House, also on Division, was built in 1854. The style is Gothic expressed in stucco and wood.

The Elks Temple, Division Street, was built in 1864 as a Spiritualist Church. The style is Roman Revival. The exterior has been altered considerably, but the massive wood interior has been preserved.

The First Presbyterian Church, on Marshall Street, was completed in 1869. The steeple is the highest in Southern Michigan at 158 feet.

The buildings on Hanchett Street display a range of architectural styles. There are buildings done in Colonial Revival, English Tudor Revival, and Queen Anne.

The Skeels Mansion, on West Pearl Street, was built in 1866. The style is Queen Anne, the foundation is cut stone. The interior features cherry woodwork, 12 foot ceilings and seven fireplaces.

The Tibbits Opera House, on South Hanchett, was built in 1882.

The Philo Crippen House, on Marshall Street, was built in 1846. The style is Greek Revival, but it is the construction methods that are remarkable. The main section of the house is made of 9" x 9" pegged hand hewn beams. The roof rafters are bark covered tamarack tree trunks. They don't build them like this anymore.

The Dickinson Homes, also on Marshall Street, were built in 1873 and 1876. The porch foundations were made from one giant piece of stone.

The homes on East Pierce Street are primarily done in the

Queen Anne style. Some say that several of these houses are haunted.

The historic homes on Grand Street were constructed in several different styles. Back in the day this truly was the grandest street in Coldwater.

The Wesleyan Methodist Church, on North Hudson Street, was built in 1852 making it the second oldest church in Coldwater. It was founded by a breakaway group who were anti slavery and wanted to assist runaway slaves.

The Masonic Temple, on East Chicago Street, was built in 1869. The original structure had 25-foot ceilings and was heated with steam. It was home to the art collection of Henry Clay Lewis and was considered the premier art collection west of New York City. This temple is home to the oldest chapter of the Eastern Star in the world.

The Wing House Museum, on South Jefferson Street, was built in 1875 in the second empire style. The exterior has authentic period colors. The museum is home to the Branch County Historical Society.

The houses on Park Place, the only boulevard in Coldwater, are seen as some of the most beautiful Queen Anne homes in the entire area.

Branch County is also known for its natural beauty. The

Chain of Lakes is a series of seven lakes including Messenger, South, Cemetery, North, Randall, Morrison and Craig lakes. There are seven connected lakes in the chain and they are full of fish of all kinds. In fact, Branch County sells more fishing licenses than any other county in Michigan. Another unique nature destination is the Alligator Sanctuary. They showcase the learning abilities of the alligators, no wrestling or anything of that sort. There are usually 100 - 150 alligators at any time. These alligators are all rescues. At the sanctuary they are healed and receive training. They all get color training so each responds to a specific color for training. They can learn their names. In fact, they hear better than dogs and can distinguish specific sounds like the difference between Ned & Ted.

There is something else rare and wonderful here. A visit to the Burlington General Store and their amazing collection isn't to be missed. The Burlington Store has a museum created from the collection of just one woman. Included among the 4000+ toys are some 1500 dolls. That makes this the largest collection of dolls in the state as far as I can tell. Three rooms, four aisles, floor to ceiling are hundreds and hundreds of dolls in mint condition. On display are Original Shirley Temple dolls, cabbage patch, Baby Thumbalina and Yosemite Sam. There is an enormous doll house that is fully decorated. The store is only open on weekends.

CROSWELL – LEXINGTON GETAWAY

Michigan was settled and developed from Fort Detroit north and west. As traffic grew on the Great Lakes, safe harbors grew in importance as well. One of those was found at Lexington. The Croswell-Lexington area was soon noted for its natural beauty and became known as a resort area. Lake Huron is the eastern boundary and the Black River is the western. Between those are beaches, trails, camping, golf courses, hotels, shops, restaurants, wineries, festivals and the towns of Croswell and Lexington. One very popular way to explore is the Croswell-Lexington Bike Path. The Bicycle Path is a perfect 5 - 6 mile ride through the country. It runs between the swinging bridge in Croswell past orchards, farms and a golf course to Lexington, where it ends at Lake Huron.

This region is well known for festivals. In fact, there are enough festivals that some plan to come back in every season of the year. Fireworks are held on the Lexington Harbor break wall in July. There is the Street Art Fair, Air Margaritaville, Lake Huron Spring Fling Fishing Tournament, the Swinging Bridge Festival, Fine Arts Festival, Thumbfest, and the Croswell Michigan Fair, with even more planned.

While it isn't an official festival, the Baby Goose Migration brings visitors to Croswell every year to cheer the baby geese as they cross the road. It happens every year and is a signal that spring has arrived in Croswell. When you see the geese returning in spring you can be sure the parade will begin. Just a few blocks from downtown, are a couple of small ponds, and a multi-use path. So many little geese are crossing the bike path going from pond to pond, that the folks in Croswell actually post a crossing guard to control traffic. It's a great show and kids of all ages gather to cheer the babies on their way.

With all this going on, one must still find some time for shopping. This is a fun time and the shopping just adds to the trip. Arts and antiques can be found in downtown Croswell. If you want to step back in time, the Lexington General Store is the place to go. Lots of great gifts, old-timey candy counter and a full made-in-Michigan section are just a part of what you will find. When you walk in you will know you are in a special shop. Friendly people pause to say hello, there is a huge variety of old-fashioned merchandise, and many items that are made in Michigan. As you go from place to place, the history of the area keeps popping up. Railroad enthusiasts will find that the Huron and Eastern Railway Co. (HESR) and its "sister" operation, the Saginaw Valley Railway Co. (SGVY) have served the "Thumb Area" of Michigan since 1986, when their first section of track was acquired from CSX Transportation. This first segment ran from Bad Axe to the end of the line, including the town of Croswell. Another historical structure, Aitkin Memorial District Library, is in Croswell. The library first opened in 1912, as the Croswell Free Library and Reading Room, in two rooms above a barber shop.

All this fun and running around will produce an appetite. I never want to slow down, so I always look for a great breakfast, Wimpy's is the place. Well known locally, I can tell you that the food is good, the service is fast, and the conversation can be colorful. The old courthouse on the square in Lexington is now a popular brewery. In Croswell, they have been going to Camm Café for years. The great food and excellent service keep me going back. I can't pass up the biscuits and gravy. If you are looking for great down home food this is the place to go.

There is something rare and wonderful here. The Croswell Swinging Bridge is the only pedestrian suspension bridge in Michigan. It was built in 1905 at an original cost of $300. It spans 139 feet. The original bridge had just two cables, which were provided by the Michigan Sugar Company, and were used to support the planks. To provide a handhold, two more cables were added at a cost of $150. In August of 2006, all 128 planks were replaced at a cost of $1,300. The Bridge originally had a sign at the west end that admonished people to "Love Ye One Another." A sign at the east entrance still reads, "Be Good To Your Mother-in-Law."

If you are having so much fun that you want to stay over, lodging options range from hotels to bed and breakfasts. One B&B even offers a tree house room.

BEULAH

IS

THE

ONLY

COMMUNITY

ON

THE

SHORES

OF

CRYSTAL

LAKE

CRYSTAL LAKE GETAWAY

The exceptionally clean, clear body of water is Crystal Lake and the charming lake side town is Beulah. Beulah beach offers hundreds of feet of soft, sandy shore with excellent swimming and it is just 1 block from all of the cool downtown shops. The beach area also has a beach house, tennis courts, a playground and parking. The Cold Creek spills into Crystal Lake adjacent to the beach and provides another avenue for swimming enjoyment. Fourth of July celebrations include watching the fireworks display over Crystal Lake from the beach.

Crystal Lake measures approximately 2.5 by 8 miles , and has a maximum depth of 165 feet. At 9,854 acres, it is Michigan's ninth largest inland lake. The watershed that feeds Crystal Lake is very small, and fertilizer and sewage outflows are minimal, leading to the exceptionally clear and beautiful water that gives this Michigan attraction its current name. With that beautiful lake at hand, it is no wonder that there are festivals going on throughout the year. Music in the Park happens every Thursday at 7:00 pm in July and August There are the Fourth of July celebrations featuring the fireworks display over Crystal Lake. There is Art In The Park in July, the Crystal Lake Team Marathon in August, the Cold Creek Bridge Walk in Beulah on Labor Day, Fall Fest in October, a Halloween Maze and Christmas Magic.

Some people arrive here on the Betsie Valley Trail. The

trail is built on the bed of the former Ann Arbor Railroad. It has 22 very scenic miles long and extends from Frankfort through Elberta and Beulah to Thompsonville. From Beulah to Frankfort it is non-motorized. All of it is excellent for bicycles and pedestrian use. From Beulah to Thompsonville (13 miles) the compacted aggregate trail is open to snowmobiles from December through March. Downtown Beulah has a full range of dining and lodging options. A local favorite is the Cold Creek Inn. The main street has gift shops, a photography shop and outfitters.

At the top of the hill, you will know which one, is the Benzie Historical Museum housed in an 1887 church building. The museum has exhibits of artifacts pertaining to Benzie County's history, including exhibits on Bruce Catton, a native of Michigan and Pulitzer Prize winner, Carferries, Logging/Agriculture, Railroads, Gwen Frostic and more. The museum also maintains the 1891 Drake School building in Honor, Michigan.

Not far away on the other side of the lake is the the oldest standing structure in Benzie County, the Point Betsie Lighthouse, built in 1858. The lighthouse stands adjacent to a public beach, consequently, it is easy to get to and has become one of the most photographed lighthouses in America. The lighthouse is positioned at the southern end of the Manitou Passage and remains in use as a navigational aid. The lighthouse is open for tours on weekends from Memorial Day to Columbus Day. Betsie Point and the Betsie River were named the Sawbill or

Merganser by the Indians. The lighthouse was built in 1857-58. The light first shone on October 20, 1858 and has been in continuous service for more than 150 years. The structure sits 52 feet above the lake and has a range of about 15 miles. The original lens, and its 1891 replacement, were of the fourth-order Fresnel design. The current light system features a modern acrylic lens from New Zealand.

This area has something else rare and wonderful in its history, the Mistake On The Lake. If not for a small miscalculation, those beautiful sandy beaches might not exist. Up to, and through the American Civil War years, Crystal Lake was known as "Cap Lake". That name was due to the frequent whitecaps visible on its surface. The surrounding area was heavily forested with steep hills. Then, in 1873, Archibald Jones had an idea. He wanted to improve his shipping business. He decided to open a channel, to connect Crystal Lake to Lake Michigan, just a few miles away. This would greatly facilitate the movement of commodities to the Great Lakes shipping ports.

The mistake Mr. Jones made, it has even been called the "Tragedy of Crystal Lake", was that he failed to recognize the differences in water levels of the two bodies of water. The lake level of Crystal Lake was higher than the level of Lake Michigan. The channel was dug according to plan. When the Crystal lake end was opened, the lake water poured into the channel, and the water level in Crystal Lake dropped. Although the project was a failure, the lowering of the lake level uncovered sandy beaches, including the current public beach at Beulah.

They like to have fun in northern Michigan, and festivals are fun. So they celebrate "Archibald Jones Day" at the Village Park every year. Activities for all ages include a walking tour of Beulah, and the waterfront area, as well as a wide variety of "Victorian era" games. There is a simulation of the lowering of the lake, as well as hearing Mr. Jones tell his side of the story. Following Mr. Jones speech, there is a sing-along and a birthday celebration, in honor of his birthday.

ESCANABA GETAWAY

U.S. Highway 2 is the route into Escanaba from north, east, and west. Lake Michigan and Little Bay De Noc are the water routes from the south. After driving through the modern development on U.S. 2, a sign across the main boulevard invites visitors to head downtown. The broad boulevard stretches from the highway all the way to the lake, the Sand Point Lighthouse, historical museum, marina, and waterfront park, whew. Along that boulevard there is plenty of parking so you can enjoy a walk through the historic architecture while checking out the unique shops. The weather cooperates more than you might think. Escanaba is in an area called the "banana belt". The "lake effect" seems to work in reverse here, they get less snow per year than Lansing.

Historic downtown can be a day trip in and of itself. Downtown is where the independent shops are. Those seeking the best wineries should make way to Leigh's Garden. Don't let the simple exterior fool you. Inside is a gorgeous wine tasting room and people who know the local wines and vineyards. Sayklly's has been satisfying those with a sweet tooth, with homemade chocolates and candies, for three generations. You can get a traditional Swedish breakfast, enjoy craft beer at the brewery, relax over a fine dining experience or get one of the best subs anywhere. The Escanaba Market Place brings fresh local products to a convenient outdoor venue.

The William Bonifas Fine Arts Center is downtown as well. It is a regional art center with art workshops, classes, theatrical production and free gallery exhibits. The works of local artists are also available at the Ludington Gallery. At the southern end of the boulevard is the Sand Point Lighthouse and the Delta County Historical Museum. The exhibits are extensive depicting: logging, shipping, Native American culture, and the railroad industry, among others.

Instead of downtown, many come here for the natural wonders that are all around. There is so much to choose from that it will require more than one trip. This area has the most freshwater shoreline in Michigan's Upper Peninsula, 200+ miles of it. There are beautiful sand beaches, marshes and wetlands for bird and wildlife viewing, and stunning limestone cliffs. The fishing here is legendary. It is so good that there are a number of professional tournaments each year. Trophy sized fish are not the only thing lurking below the water's surface, over 30 sunken ships can be found in the nearby waters. Even a drive through the northern hardwoods of the Hiawatha National Forest for a color tour can make for a day trip.

One nature area that is often overlooked is the Hemlock Cathedral. Just a few miles east on County Road 513 toward Stonington is the Little Bay de Noc Recreation Area. Take a walk on the Maywood History Trail and you will reach an area called the Hemlock Cathedral.

This stand of Hemlocks survived the lumber boom at the turn of the last century. Some of these majestic trees are more than 300 years old. The trail in is only a half mile or so. The quiet and sense of wonder will stay with you long after you leave. The name Maywood Trail dates from the 1800s when this stand was first dubbed The Hemlock Cathedral.

While exploring and discovering, consider a stop at the Ten Mile Creek Forge a few miles away in Bark River. Ten Mile Creek Forge is usually described as a pottery and lighting gift shop. It actually holds original work by about 30 artists. It is where George Potvin works his magic at the forge and blacksmith shop. Artwork of local artists includes Irish crystal, jewelry, bath & beauty, perfumes, colognes, hand-blown glass, stained glass, hand-made purses, raku, smoke-fire pottery and beautiful, functional pottery, hand scrimshaw, wood and soapstone carving, watercolor, photography, quilting, basketry, candles and more. That is just in the gift shop.

Out in the forge, George Potvin creates knives and scrimshaw work that is recognized world-wide. He hand-forges his blades and does all of his own heat-treating. He has created cable Damascus as well as traditional Damascus. Some knives are purposely primitive, while some are like polished jewels. They are always ready to use or to keep for your collection, or to give as treasured gifts. All knives come with hand-made sheaths that are designed, fitted and sewn to fit each individual knife. For handle material, George uses exotic woods from around the world, or indigenous birds eye or tiger maple. He even creates scrimshaw handles on indigenous deer antlers.

Festivals in Escanaba are another way to learn about this area. There's a classic car cruise, events on the dock, several fishing related events an tournaments, and Uptoberfest for celebrating color tour time. The National Trappers Association convention comes to town every winter.

There is something else rare and wonderful here. Nearby is a spot where the Monarch Butterflies pause on their fall migration. The road to Stonington, Route 513, ends after 17 miles at Stonington Point. Every autumn, during the last two weeks of August, and the first two weeks of September, Monarch Butterflies appear at Stonington Point. Here, they gather in the trees and on the bushes, by the tens of thousands. When the winds are right, they take off in fantastic numbers, forming enormous clouds of butterflies. The migration flight heads south across Lake Michigan, across Green Bay, and on, to their winter home in the mountains of Mexico. A flight that will require about five weeks.

Some say that the Monarchs gather on the Garden Peninsula, and some do, but the real action is at Stonington Point. The specific day the butterflies arrive on the point is unpredictable, but many flocks do land during the last two weeks in August, and the first two weeks in September. If you visit the peninsula during those weeks, and they are not there, just come back every day or so. The point itself is several acres, with a 3 story lighthouse, that is open if you want to climb to the top. There are several picnic areas, interpretive signs, and, if you are there on the right day, thousands of Monarch butterflies.

With so much to see and do, you might want to stay over. There is a range of lodging options from which to choose. Local guides and maps are available at the DDA visitors center on Ludington Street just off the boulevard.

FENTON

WAS

NAMED

AS

THE

RESULT

OF

A

POKER

GAME

FENTON GETAWAY

My first visit to Fenton was a spur of the moment trip. It happened like this, I had ordered a sandwich at a small coffee shop in Goodrich, Michigan. I was blown away by how delicious the bread was. I asked if they made their own and they said "No, they ordered bread from a baking company known as Crust, in Fenton, Michigan". Months later I was near Fenton, and had an hour to kill, so I decided to go visit this bakery. The only other clue I had was that I had heard that Fenton had a really cool map, with a Walking Tour laid out, for downtown. Right on the edge of the downtown district is the Chamber of Commerce office. They have lots of visitor information, and free copies of that great map. As I drove around downtown trying to locate Crust, I became aware that I had arrived in a pretty special town. I was seeing all kinds of sculpture and other art work scattered around. There was great architecture and really cool looking shopping districts. Once I had the map of the Walking Tour, I found Crust, and immediately, began making plans to return, park, and tour the whole downtown.

One of the attractions of downtown Fenton is the architecture, including the Community Center building, which was nominated as one of the most significant structures in Michigan. The design is the work of Eliel Saarinen. He was a Finnish architect, known for his art nouveau buildings, in the early years of the 20th century. The building was considered way ahead of its time and architectural students still journey to Fenton just to explore this building. The poker table sculpture in front of the Community Center tells the story of how Fenton got its name. The story goes that citizens couldn't agree on a name for the city so the possible honorees decided to settle the matter like gentlemen. They had a game of poker on August 24, 1837. The sculpture depicts three men, William M. Fenton, Robert LeRoy, and Benjamin Rockwell. Some people say Mr. Dibble was in the game. In any event, Mr. Fenton won and the community adopted his name. As a consolation prize, Robert LeRoy had his name given to LeRoy Street. Mr. LeRoy later built the Fenton Hotel, which is said to be haunted. There is an empty seat at the poker table just for photo ops.

Another way to tour this area is a float trip on the Shiawassee River. There is an outfitter in Fenton, but they don't offer float trips. In Linden, about a 10 minute drive west, you can rent a kayak. They can take you to Holly, about 10 minutes east, you put in at the river there, and away you go. In a short while, you will arrive in downtown Fenton, and almost everything you are looking for will be within a couple of blocks of the river park. When done in town, just hop into the kayak and float on down to Linden. If you don't want a river float, people also kayak on the mill pond. The map and other information available at the Chamber Office on Adelaide St. will provide directions to the nature areas and trails.

Downtown Fenton has every kind of dining option you

could ask for, from known chains to some of the best artisan dining experiences in southeast Michigan. There is casual dining, fine dining, a Japanese Bistro, and a new Italian Bistro. Foodies are going to have their hands full trying to cover it all. A couple of these places shouldn't be missed. Crust was what brought me here. They have way more than just bread. They have full day time and dinner menus, everything is mouth-watering. Then there is the Laundry. Depending on who is describing the place, it is referred to as everything from European to Trendy. It doesn't matter what you call it, the food is awesome. The Laundry serves breakfast, lunch or dinner. They have an extensive menu with unique items and great specials. The sandwiches are stuffed and they use breads from Crust, so you know you are going to be happy. In addition there is a full bar, and a range of non-alcoholic, hot and cold beverages. Another real treat downtown is found at El Topo. What you do, is go in, make your way to the back and locate the Pringles vending machine, push the button to choose original. When you do, a door opens to the Speakeasy where they concentrate on old school cocktails, no password required.

While it isn't located in downtown Fenton, some people travel here just to visit the Fenton Winery & Brewery. They are a micro-brewery with the brewing going on right in the tap room. I can tell you that the house stout is as good as you will find. They are very friendly, are known for their pizzas, and are even pet friendly during the warm months, in their outdoor seating area. Be sure to say hello to Hans.

The food is great and the architecture is noteworthy The shopping is yet another attraction that draws visitors in the know. That map with the Walking Tour is also at several other locations. One spot is a very cool shop in the "old town" district called Yesterday's Treasures. You will notice the unusual exterior eventually, so this is as good a place to start your tour as any. Just be aware that when you go inside for "the map" of the Walking Tour, you will almost certainly end up shopping the entire store. Another business, Gerych's, is as much a local attraction as it is a shop. It's a flower store, gift shop, and event rental business and has served the town for many, many years. It is a good place to stop if you are looking for a Fenton souvenir.

Thousands of people travel to Fenton for the festivals. Among the events in town are the Community Expo, the Fenton Freedom Festival on the 4th of July, with a parade, afternoon festival and evening fireworks. Also in July is the annual Art Walk. Late in the summer it is Taste In Fenton. December holidays are celebrated with Jinglefest. Activities include Jinglejog walk/run, ice sculpture display, music, shopping, horse drawn wagon rides, evening parade and fireworks! Getaway destinations like this are the result of community pride and organization. The Fenton Chamber of Commerce not only provides information, and sponsored this chapter, they also invested in Fenton by buying a building that also hosts 4 business tenants. In addition they organize a majority of the events in town.

Trails are one of the reasons that Fenton is there to enjoy today. Seems that in the early 1800s Clark Dibble was making the trek from Shiawassee to Grumlaw. Not surprisingly he became confused in the wilderness and ended up on the White Lake Trail. In this area he turned north and found a spot on the Shiawassee River where several Indian trails intersected. The spot was so beautiful that he decided to stay and Dibbleville, Fenton today, was established. Hidden away, north of downtown, is a beautiful nature preserve that offers easy trails through the dense forest. Inside the Dauner Martin Nature Sanctuary there are no sand dunes, rushing rivers, or sun-drenched beaches. There are more than 150 acres of woods and wetlands with 4.5 miles of walking paths. There's a large pine grove and stands of hardwoods. There are four main loops in the trail system. When winter ends, the wildflowers bloom and in the autumn the fall colors are second to none.

There is something rare and wonderful in the "old town" section of Fenton. There is an independent, full service book store, Fenton's Open Book . The selection is going to surprise shoppers, and this is the place to get real information about the history of Fenton. They have books on that poker game and the history of the settlement when it was known as Dibbleville and all that was here, were a few houses and a couple of sawmills. Fenton's Open Book is the place to stop if you need contact information for the Historical Museum.

GROSSE ILE GETAWAY

Grosse Ile is a "Down River" island where the Detroit River enters Lake Erie. It is as different from Detroit as it is possible to imagine and, there are 10 square miles to explore. Grosse Ile is an island where the pace of life is slower. The top speed for autos is 35 mph, most places keep it at 25 mph. That alone makes this a bicycle and dog friendly place. In 2016, Grosse Ile Township was named the safest city in Michigan. The main "downtown" area is Macomb Street. There are other shops and historic destinations all over the island, all connected by trails, bike paths and excellent roads. If you want to make the most of your time on the island, make your way to the Grosse Ile Pet & Garden Center on Macomb. The shop is jammed with an impressive selection of gifts and souvenirs. As you would expect everything for the garden, and those beloved pets, is at hand. Most importantly, they have maps and brochures, with all the info you need to explore Grosse Ile and, they know all about the festivals and events that are so much a part of life here. Without their support this getaway wouldn't have been possible.

Grosse Ile is located in the heart of the Detroit International Wildlife Refuge. Whether driving, hiking, or biking, here are some of gems that are all time favorites: Bird Sanctuary on Thorofare Canal, Gibralter Bay, East River Historical District, Macomb Street District, Westcroft Botanical Gardens, and more. There are miles of bike trails, nature trails, acres of open spaces and woods, and those breath taking river views everywhere you go.

With biking being so prevalent here, it isn't surprising that there is an amazing bicycle museum that has extremely rare bicycles in pristine condition. Cycling is a way of life here, and several events revolve around the sport. The Lazy Ride is a monthly event, held during the summer months, just to take a leisurely ride around the island. Glow Roll is an electric light bicycle parade. Tour De Ile is a major event at the end of summer. Hundreds gather to cycle around the island and to historical destinations off island. The Baroudeur Bike Tour is a 100 mile ride through Detroit and Downriver locations. Grosse Ile hosts a rest area for that event. If all that weren't enough, Grosse Ile is included in the Iron Belle Trail.

It isn't all bicycling. There are nature trails, open green spaces, and acres of woods. If you are looking for an easy walking trail, with a wide variety of flowers and plant life, you can't do better than the trail through the Westcroft Botanical Gardens. Westcroft is the oldest farm in Michigan still owned and operated by the same family. They got started in 1776. The walking trail winds through four and half acres of trees, shrubs, evergreens and hybrid azaleas created by the family. These gardens are beautiful, the trail is great, and a lot of it is in the shade, making it very pleasant even on the hottest of days. Gibraltar Bay and the bird sanctuary provide even more natural beauty.

With its' beginnings so soon after the birth of the nation, it is no surprise that the history of Grosse Ile is written in its architecture and preserved in its' museums. July 6, 1776, two days after the Declaration of Independence was signed. That is the date, when William and Alexander Macomb signed an agreement with the Potawatomi Indians, to take ownership of the island. They began establishing their homesteads almost immediately. For information about the Treaty Tree and the Wonder Well, visit the Historical Society or the Pet and Garden Center. They made this chapter possible. The Historical Society keeps its' archives in the 1873 Customs House, behind the Railroad House Museum. Both structures contain huge collections of artifacts from island history. The Grosse Ile lighthouse began service in 1894. It lit the way for vessels traveling from Grosse Ile to the Canadian shore.

There are other interesting places to visit scattered across the island. Centennial Farm has the horses, a fairy garden and the Butterfly Gardens. Sunrise Beach has convenient bike parking and stairs to water. It is a favorite launch spot for kayaks to make way to Stony Island. The Grosse Ile Recreation Area is another spot favored for kayaking. The Hickory Nature Conservancy has lots of history on Hickory Island, and Gibraltar Bay is a beautiful nature preserve.

One place that is a must visit, is the Gibraltar Alpaca Farm. Part of the tour is the owners calling in the alpacas. When you walk out of the barn, there may not be many alpacas visible. They start to signal the missing alpacas and, in a short time, here they come in a hilarious alpaca stampede. They know that it is going to be good. They actually have a look of great anticipation on their funny alpaca faces. They gather around looking for treats and poking their noses in everything. The farm operates a gift shop full of woolen items made from alpaca shearings. If you make a purchase, you can even get a picture of the alpaca that produced the wool your item came from.

The dining scene is as varied as the rest of the island attractions. You can get great shrimp from downriver and barbecue near the water. You can opt for fine dining or head for the spot the where locals gather. The Airport Inn established in 1942 has some of the best old style pizza in the area. There are only a few lodging options on the island. The Pilot House, at the Naval Air Station, now serves as one option.

There is something rare and wonderful here. For something completely different, check out the Old Spokes Home of Grosse Ile, a bicycle museum. Among the treasures housed inside is an Evenrude 1936 Stream Flow, only a half dozen exist in the world. Old Spokes is open by appointment.

HISTORIC SHIAWASSEE GETAWAY

Two themes keep repeating as you explore the Michigan region known as, Historic Shiawassee, the natural beauty along the Shiawassee River, and the history of the railroads. Places to visit include an Historic Village, Castle, Train Depot, Art Exhibits, Performing Arts Theatre, and a museum with the largest sleigh and carriage collection in the mid-west. As you travel from town to town, there are historic homes, vintage barns, miles of trails, and a number of nature preserves.

Each of the principle towns in Shiawasee County offers shopping and dining options, and each has one or more unique historical destinations to explore. Corunna has the Historical Village. Durand has the Union Station and Railroad History Museum. Owosso has Curwood Castle Park. There is more to discover in each community. For those who love Michigan history, Historic Shiawassee is a destination to return to again and again. Visiting the various destinations is very nearly a tour of the entire history of the state of Michigan. The Historical Sites Tour is an eye-opening way to explore the area. Here are the high points of the tour.

Corunna Historical Village – If you ever get the urge to find out what the "good old days" were really like, Corunna is the town to visit. The Historical Village there has created a destination that brings that time to life. You can experience what life was like with no running water, no electricity, and no automobiles. Heck, back then they didn't even have facebook, OMG. Life was different. It was a quieter time, with a slower pace. A visit here will give you a good idea what the "good old days" were really like.

Curwood Castle – Between 1922 and 1923, James Oliver Curwood built the castle to serve as his writing studio. He was an early conservationist and a celebrated novelist. His work is so enduring that more than 200 motion pictures have been inspired by his writings. The "Castle" sits on the banks of the Shiawassee River within the grounds of Curwood Castle Park. Also within the parks' 8 acres, on the Shiawassee River, are the Shiawassee Arts Center, Comstock Pioneer Cabin, Woodard Paymaster Building, Walk of History, Heritage Bridge, Miner Walkway. Curwood Castle is the 7th most visited historical site in Michigan.

DeVries Nature Conservancy – Carriage and Sleigh Museum – Here are preserved carriages, buggies, sleighs and others, nearly 30 of them, making this one of the largest collections in the mid-west. Some of the vehicles on display were manufactured nearby, at the old Owosso Carriage and Sleigh Company, in the early 1900s. They make great use of some sleighs, offering winter rides on the trails of the nature conservancy trails.

Durand Union Station and Michigan Railroad History Museum – This depot has become one of the most photographed train stations in the U.S. The museum houses exhibits featuring photos and artifacts from the glory days of Durand's railroading past.

Shiawassee County Historical Museum – The museum maintains collections of written records and artifacts from across the entire county. Group tours are welcome.

Steam Railroading Institute – This organization works to preserve the knowledge and skills necessary to operate steam locomotives, and to tell the story of the impact railroading had on the development of Michigan. This is where you can book a color tour train ride. The color tour is aboard our vintage passenger coaches pulled by a Great Lakes Central diesel locomotive. Enjoy a ride through Northern Michigan and get pictures that can't be found any other way.

Nature lovers will have their hands full trying to decide what to do first. A really fun option is to float the Shiawassee River. Trips are available from Bancroft in the south to Henderson in the north, with lots of short trips in between. Along a 100+ miles, the Shiawassee River meanders across the county, through towns, historic sites, and wilderness. The Friends of the Shiawassee River have constructed a half dozen canoe launches between Geeck Road County Park and Henderson Road County Park. This is a gentle, Class 1, waterway so it is accessible for almost anyone. The various eco-systems include lakes, a narrow section where the banks are close by, and unique a swampy fen area. Those wetlands are the result of underground alkaline springs and are home to some rare species of wildlife. Other nature areas that make for a fun getaway include, the Miner River Walk, DeVries Nature Conservancy, Geo-Caching, and miles of hiking and biking trails.

With all this history and natural beauty as part of day to day life, it's no surprise that there are festivals, celebrations, and events, all year long. In no particular order, here are a few festivals that are as good a reason as any for a Shiawassee Getaway. Artwalk Owosso, July 4th Corunna, Curwood Festival, Durand Railroad Days, Bike Week, Shiawassee County Fair, Historic Home Tour, North Pole Express. There are several more, seems like something is going on all the time.

There is also something rare and wonderful here. The Pere Marquette No. 1225 is the crown jewel of the collection at the Steam Railroading Institute. This is one of the last of the giant, powerful steam locomotives. Old 1225 became famous as the "Real" Polar Express in the popular movie. The movie people needed something authentic so, this engine was literally saved from the scrap heap. You can enjoy train excursions throughout the year. The most popular is the "North Pole Express" excursion offered in November and December.

HURON JEWEL GETAWAY

If you are looking for a getaway that is different, how about a day trip on a Great Lakes Schooner? The Huron Jewel is the first schooner to be built and launched on the Great Lakes in more than fifty years. Historically, the "schooner" was a sailing ship with two or more masts, the foremast being smaller than the mainmast. These tall ships were ideal for work requiring speed, windward ability, and ease of handling. The Huron Jewel embodies all of these characteristics and, she is a Bed & Breakfast as well. The salon will seat 10, there are two queen berths and 2 single births. There is full headroom below decks for someone 6' tall. A full kitchen and traditional ice box, which is easier to keep cold than a refrigerator, add to the comfort. The creators of this experience, and builders of the schooner, Hugh and Julie Covert, put it this way - *Sailing the Dream on the Great Lakes* - "Memories are made when you take part in life - take the wheel, hoist the sales, and ride the wind aboard the Schooner Huron Jewel." The Huron Jewel, the fastest tall ship on the Great Lakes, can be found at Yacht Haven on Drummond Island.

The Huron Jewel offers a quick and easy getaway that will fit for any schedule. The boat has a shallow draft of only about four feet. The upshot is that they can sail very close to the islands so guests can really get a feel for the beauty of this region. As an "at dock B&B", they have a sunset cruise of about two hours and guests stay aboard overnight at the dock. A cruise of two hours consists of a visit to the Harbor Island National Wildlife Refuge, Sturgeon Bay, and Potagannissing Bay. Another option is a four hour cruise that includes the destinations in the two hour cruise plus a go by of the lighthouse. Both of these cruises offer great picture taking and the possibility of passing a Great Lakes freighter. The vessel is available for custom cruises and is capable of sailing great distances, even to the Caribbean.

The Huron Jewel also offers an all day and a two day, "Sail Around Drummond" cruise. Depending on weather, as always, you sail out of Yacht Haven and out to Potagannissing Bay. The sail then goes past the Alvar at Maxton Plains, and close up visit to the Fossil Ledges. The cruise continues to Glen Cove, Pilot Harbor, past Marblehead, Shelter Island and Scammon Cove. A check of the weather, and the cruise continues on to Cream City Point for shipwrecks and a sail by of the lighthouse. Guests sleep on board beneath starry skies and dream of the gourmet breakfast, made from scratch, that will be served up in the morning.

Last trip of the season leaves port on the Wednesday after Labor Day. Here is Julies description of the Captain's Choice Cruise to the North Channel and Georgian Bay. "Sail with us in the beautiful North Channel and Georgian Bay to the Captain's favorite and special anchorages, such as Bear Drop and the Pool, during this amazing 12 day trip. The sights and anchorages are too many to name, but we'll definitely be stopping in the historic towns of Little Current and Killarney, the breathtaking Baie Fine, along with parts of the French and Bad Rivers. We'll sail past lighthouses and past hundreds of islands. Excursions ashore will allow for hikes, plant walks and photography of some of the most scenic areas in this region." Accommodations and all meals on board are included. Alcoholic beverages are BYOB. Valid passports are mandatory.

Drummond Island, most any destination can be described as "unique", but this hidden treasure really can be designated as a unique paradise. It is the second largest freshwater island in the United States and the eighth largest in the world. Even the short list is impressive: 150 miles of shoreline, 30 bays and coves, 34 inland lakes, 100 miles of ORV trails comprising one of the largest closed loop trail systems for off road - ATV / ORV exploration in the U.S., 70 miles of groomed snowmobile trails, more than a dozen shipwrecks, 58 neighboring islands, a lighthouse and a ferry ride.

The Huron Jewel is 78' feet overall and 60' feet on the deck. The boat has 12,000 pounds of ballast. Sailing is augmented by two, 100 horsepower diesel engines. The main boom is 40'; they employ traditional rigging with blocks and pulleys. As part of the experience passengers are allowed to raise and lower sails and steer the boat under supervision. Coast Guard regulations impose a limit of six passengers.

There is something else rare and wonderful here. A natural ecosystem occurs on Drummond Island, known locally as the Maxton Plains. This flatland area is a unique grassland, called an alvar. Alvars are extremely rare plant communities existing on limestone bedrock. Alvars are only found in partss of Canada, the United States and Sweden. These plains are grasslands growing on very thin soil consisting of bulrush sedge and ragwort, prairie dropseed, prairie smoke, and Indian paintbrush. There are even fields of Prairie Smoke sprouting up through the cracks in the rocks. Another unusual feature of alvars is that trees tend to grow in straight lines following the soil filled cracks in the bed rock. The Maxton Plains on Drummond Island are some of the largest remaining in North America at about 2 miles by 4 miles. The interpretive signs will enrich the experience.

KALKASKA GETAWAY

Kalkaska is a place where people who love the out-of-doors gather in every season. In the immediate region are more than 70 lakes and the headwaters of two important rivers, the Boardman and the Manistee. Spring is welcome every year with the National Trout Festival. Winter is celebrated with the Iceman Cometh Race. Thousands of racers from dozens of countries roll across the frozen country side in a 29 mile mountain bike race. Summer offers up everything in between. The Kalkaska Winterfest is the largest sprint sled dog race in the continental United States. As many as 100 teams compete in a variety of events. One very popular event is the skijorer race. This is an event where the dogs pull racers on cross country skis. Other events include a dog pull competition, and a Recliner Race, winter demolition derby. Kalkaska has been the center for exploring "up north" since the lumbering days. Nearby is Seven Bridges Park called the "Jewel of Kalkaska County". Rugg Pond is a local favorite for an afternoon picnic, a short nature walk or a quick break to try to catch delicious trout. The Leetsville ORV Trail offers 20+ miles of trail riding.

There are attractions in town as well. Cherry Street Market is filled to bursting with fresh pure Michigan farm goods, locally grown products and lots of Michigan made goodies, the market is open May - November; locally owned and operated. Running for about a city block along the road front will be stacks of planters, flowers, fruits and vegetables, just begging you to stop for a quick look see. When you start wandering it won't be long until you find the garden and statuary area in the back and that area is enormous too. As if all this isn't enough, the market also operates a fantastic bakery/deli filled with delicious treats.

The old railroad depot is now the Historical Museum. One of the unusual exhibits inside is an Elmer Car. Elmer Johnson built bicycles for the Montgomery Ward Company and also built four cars, in his machine shop, on S. Cedar Street in Kalkaska. The car, known as the "Elmer", was built by hand in 1898 for Henry Stover, a druggist in Kalkaska.

You can't really talk about Kalkaska without describing the National Trout Festival. It is held annually to celebrate the opening of trout season. The National Trout Festival has been running for more than 75 years. It goes on for nearly a week every April. Opening Ceremonies get it started at the Trout Memorial including the Trout King and Queen Coronation. Past festivals have included a carnival, craft show, trout fishing contests and a parade.

A day trip to one of the nature areas is a very good reason to stop in Kalkaska. Just a bit outside of town on Valley Road is Rugg Pond. This Michigan treasure is result of the construction of the Kalkaska Light and Power Company in 1904. The pond is formed where two branches of the Rapid River meet. Stories are told that Ernest Hemingway spent a night fishing here. I like this spot for a number of reasons. It is on a scenic drive toward Rapid River. There are trout in this body of water. From where you park it is only a walk of 50 yards and you are fishing and you can fish effectively from the banks, perfect for travelers looking for a half hour vacation. Finally, it isn't shown on most maps under its real name so it isn't packed with people all the time; just love it.

Another spot is the Seven Bridges Park. When you get out of your car, the first thing you are aware of, is the sound of tumbling water. Just a few feet down the rustic path you come to the first bridge. By the time you pass the first bridge on the Seven Bridges Park Trail you will have left the everyday world behind and entered a world of tranquil natural beauty. Locally known as the "Jewel of Kalkaska County", the Seven Bridges Park is best known for its rustic wooden bridges that cross the Rapid River and its adjacent tributaries. The trail is only a mile long and is almost entirely forested. Along the streams and river, wildflowers will add their special beauty to scene. This river happens to be a blue ribbon trout stream, and the Seven Bridges area has over one mile of river frontage. It isn't unusual to encounter trout fishermen along the patchwork of interconnecting streams. The paths are nicely groomed, the boardwalks are well maintained, and the bridges are in excellent repair. While a few miles from anywhere, the music of the running water, the shaded pathways, and profusion of wetland wildflowers, make this spot one of my favorite 15 minute vacations, while traveling the back roads.

There is something else rare and wonderful here, but you have to come at the right time of year. Every June the Speeder Cars arrive. The speeder car excursion runs from Cadillac to Petoskey with a stop in Kalkaska at Chalker Park. When the speeder cars reach the park, kids of all ages are gathered to climb aboard. Speeders, or Maintenance of Way cars, are railroad motorcars that were formerly used on railroads around the world by track inspectors and work crews to move quickly to and from work sites. Although it is slow compared to a train or car, it is called speeder because it is faster than a human-powered vehicle such as a handcar.

LES CHENEAUX GETAWAY

Les Cheneaux is a destination that may be different from any other in Michigan. Here it is all about the nature preserves, the water and those fantastic islands. The region is informally known as "Land Of Waters". It is populated by two historic villages, Cedarville and Hessel. In and around those towns is where the shops, museums, and art galleries are found. This is an area that is about natural wonders and the activities to be enjoyed out of town. Long empty beaches, shorelines strewn with giant boulders, and vast pristine forests are the real attractions.

The area is often referred to as "one of the last great places". In addition to the natural splendor, Les Cheneaux is famous for its Culinary School, the Boat Building School, and the Antique Wooden Boat Show. The 12 miles of shore on Lake Huron, with Cedarville and Hessel, are where the festivals are held. Those include Music and Art Dockside in July and Art In The Park in September. More about festivals and the local arts scene can be found at the Visitors Center, the Arts Council, the Old Shell Gallery and Pickle Point.

Les Cheneaux has always been bonded to the woods and waters, since the late 19th century. For 150 years, a few knew about this place. While tourism has contributed to modernization and expansive growth to the west, here are islands, unspoiled forests and spectacular waters. The Les Cheneaux Archipelago consists of 36 islands with the attendant coves, channels and hidden shorelines. The villages of Cedarville and Hessel welcome visitors year round and preserve the lifestyle and maritime history unique to this part of Mackinac County.

Visitors new to the Les Cheneaux are going to need directions to fully enjoy all the things are are to do. The list of activities includes but is not limited to: biking & hiking, bird watching, camping, paddle sports of all kinds, festivals, fishing & hunting, golfing, historic museums, nature preserves, ORV & ATV, skiing & snowshoeing, snowmobiling, Island hopping, freighter watching, and trails for finding herbs, wildflowers and mushrooms. Nature preserves are found on the mainland and throughout the islands. Just scratching the surface, here are some of my favorites.

The largest is the Aldo Leopold Nature Preserve on Marquette Island. It includes1,600+ acres, nearly 4 miles of Lake Huron shoreline. There is a trail from north to south, though parts can be wet in some seasons. The Seiberling Stewart Nature Preserve is also on Marquette Island with a nice trail from Marquette Bay to the south side of the island. The Cearville Bay Nature Preserve on La Salle Island is a five acre nature area and is accessible by water only. Little LaSalle Preserve is over 90+ acres accessible by water only and is so remote that a guide is recommended. Government Island includes a campground along with beaches, walking trails and gorgeous views of Lake Huron. On the mainland the options are nearly endless. The Woollam Nature Preserve has a mile long trail that leads to the shoreline. This preserve is a hot destination for birders during the spring songbird migration in May.

At the other end of the spectrum is the Low Springer Trail. It is really a complex of old logging roads that is a favorite with orv enthusiasts. Search Bay features beaches and rustic camping. The views are spectacular. Amazingly, during the September color time, I have gone there and found that I had the whole place to myself. Also in the Hiawatha National Forest is the Trefry Trail. This is Forest Road 3433, an easy gravel two track that leads into the wilderness with several walking trails branching off. These trails are not well marked and a compass will be really handy. If you love winter sports, the Bay City Lake Trail is known for excellent cross-country skiing and snowshoeing trails. East of Hessel is the Mackinac Bay Preserve, notable for the handicap-accessible ramp overlooking the marsh. Just down the road from there is the Beaver Dam Sanctuary. These are a few of the options, a full guide is available at the Visitors Center and Pickle Point, including important seasonal notes.

Birding is a favorite activity out in the channels and on the islands. The Les Cheneaux Area is included as one of five unique zones of the North Huron Birding Trail. This region is on a migratory route. The marshes, wetlands and sedge meadows provide food and nesting habitat for more than 250 species of birds. Bird watching locations include Cedarville Bay Park, Search Bay National Forest Campground, Birge Nature Preserve, Derby Nature Preserve, Woollam Nature Preserve and Prentiss Bay. Naturally there are all kinds of water birds like loons, osprey, ducks and terns. There are alos warblers, verios and those very cool pileated woodpeckers..

Another way to visit is via the Les Cheneaux Water Trail. This was one of the first water trails developed in Michigan and is still considered among the very best. The trail is more than 75 miles long from St. Ignace in the west to the St. Mary's River in the east. These waters were vital to the daily life of Native Americans and were eventually used by French explorers making their way from the DeTour Passage to the Straits of Mackinac. The Michigan Nature Conservancy gives this water trail high marks and considers it as an excellent way to explore one of the "Last Great Places" in the Western Hemisphere. The trail has been navigated since prehistory by paddlers. Even though we find power boats and sail boats plying the channels and shorelines. All of this can be comfortably explored by paddling the trail. The pristine marshes and wetlands, limestone shorelines and karst features, with their populations rare and endangered species are there to be enjoyed. If you don't bring your own equipment there are outfitters and guides in town. Camping sites of every kind and small cabin resorts are located along the trail.

Two museums house artifacts, exhibits and preserve the history of the region. The Les Cheneaux Historical Museum is comprised of two buildings, one, a log cabin, depicts the early days of settlement when lumbering was the primary. The other building is quite modern and shows the changes that have taken place in the communities over the years, the transition from lumbering to the tourism of today.

The Maritime Museum, housed in a 1920's boathouse, is home to displays of vintage boats, marine artifacts, antique outboard motors, historic photos of area boating, a boat building workshop, and a gift shop. On the grounds is a replica of a Mackinaw boat, the standard means of transportation before roads were improved. Its double-ended design allowed boats to be easily beached in storms. Inside, the exhibits will entertain and educate. There are artifacts from the past that aren't easy to find in any other museum.

There is something else rare and wonderful here. There are still a few places where the smelt run as the ice leaves the shoreline. While these tasty fish no longer run in the legendary numbers of a few decades ago, they are still here, if you know where to go. Getting the smelt required going out into the wilderness and wild places at night. Even if you aren't going smelt dipping, there is a place where you can relive the spirit of the past. Out on the south end of Long Island is a cove with a long stretch of cedar and spruce along the shoreline. This spot was known to the Chippewa as, kauk ge nah gwah minishe, as it is shaped like a minnow. Stories of awesome smelt runs are still told there, around campfires at moon rise.

LEWISTON GETAWAY

Lewiston is the kind of place you go when you seek unspoiled wilderness. Lewiston is located in the northeast area of Lower Michigan 25 miles northeast of Grayling and 25 miles southeast of Gaylord. The area is surrounded by forests like the Grayling State Forest Area, Pigeon River Country, and the Atlanta State Forest. Around 1935 the town developed as a resort area and continues as such today. Lewiston is a nature lovers paradise. The town sits on the shore of East Twin Lake with more than 40 other lakes nearby. A short drive in any direction takes you into the forest, or Elk country or Kirtland's Warbler country. There are numerous hiking and skiing trails in the forest where the bald eagles live, plus the snow mobile trails which are groomed for winter. The combination of natural beauty and small town hospitality is hard to resist. So, if you are looking for pure sparkling waters, pristine forest trails and pine scented wilderness air, Lewiston is just the hidden treasure you are seeking.

Another reason for a getaway to Lewiston is the festivals. There is something going on here every season. Spring kicks off with a Morel Mushroom Festival which includes guided hunts. Car Show and Cruise is an annual summer event since 1991, great cars, arts and crafts, and a Saturday night cruise. Timberfest, always in August, is a celebration of the lumber era heritage that is in evidence all through the area.

The Bike Color Tour is a ride through the changing forests on winding back roads every September. Hundreds of bikes gather at the Lewiston Hotel to group up and renew old friendships. The unspoiled wilderness and quality winding roads, make this is a prime choice for color tours. This is also where the other bridge walk is, the Lovells Bridge Walk in nearby Lovell's. Walkers of all ages come to Lewiston for a couple days, just to participate in the Lovell's Bridge Walk. While not as busy as the walk across the Mackinac Bridge, attendees insist it is a lot more fun. Be sure to get plenty of rest before the big event. The bridge spans the north branch of the Au Sable River which must be every bit of 60 feet.

Winter has its own outdoor activities cross country skiing, snowshoeing, snowmobiling and ice fishing. There is also an indoor activity in Lewiston, curling. There are only a handful of curling facilities scattered across Michigan. This excellent and modern facility is located just a block from downtown. The interior is beautifully done, they offer two complete courts, and all of the equipment you need to enjoy the sport. During the winter outside groups can rent the club. A typical two hour rental includes full instruction, all equipment and a fun curling session.

Just on the edge of town is the Buttles Trail System. This is a special place as it is a foot traffic only area. That is unique for an area that has some of the most extensive snowmobile and orv trail systems in Michigan. Buttles is set aside for cross country skiing, snow shoeing and all season hiking.

With all of these outdoor activities at hand, a guy might need to get his equipment serviced. My experience is that boats, Rvs, and bikes all have a tendency to require service or accessories. In addition, one sometimes needs directions to a specific trail or fishing spot. I always head for SUN & SNOW, a block from the light. They service everything that is a recreational vehicle, have all the accessories, and can provide those all important directions and tips about the surrounding nature destinations.

It isn't all elk and fishing around here. There are cool antique shops and gift shops. There is also a genuine treasure in downtown, the Kneeland Gallery at 2820 Kneeland St. The Kneeland Street Gallery is dedicated to supporting Michigan artists. The Gallery will usually have the work of more than 40 artists on display. The mix changes regularly because Marilyn, the owner/artist is tireless in her search for talent. The variety of arts includes; painting, pottery, quilted items, photography, woodworking (furniture, chain saw sculpture, wood turning), jewelry, metal, and much more, really, much more.

From fine dining out at the Garland Resort to a simple ice cream stand, you won't go hungry in Lewiston. The Redwood Steak House is a dinner destination with one of the best Ribeye steaks I have found. The Lewiston Hotel is a favorite gathering place and has been for generations. Friendly people and great food keep us going back over and over. In addition to steaks, seafood, and salads, they serve up one of the top burgers you can find anywhere in Michigan. This is also the place to be, if you plan to join the September Color Tour Run. There will be bikes everywhere. The Lewiston Hotel is located in the heart of Northern Michigan's great outdoors and close to all it has to offer. They have 15 clean comfortable rooms with a restaurant and lounge under the same roof, so you can spend more time enjoying the north! The Lewiston Hotel is the headquarters for the Bike Color Tour every September.

If you are traveling as group, the Woods & Wildlife Vacation Rental, might be the best option. It is a 2800 square foot home, fully remodeled, in a beautiful country setting. The home has been fully stocked all appliances including dishwasher all linens, pots & pans, blender, toaster, coffee pot,microwave, dish washer, crock pot much more. The lakes and trails are just minutes away so, you can take your time to plan and enjoy your vacation or gathering.

There is rare and wonderful wildlife right on the edge of town. Kirtland's Warbler, a member of the wood warbler family, nests in a few counties in Michigan, in Wisconsin, in Ontario. It wasn't until 1996 that any nests were found more than 60 miles from this region. Just a few miles south of Lewiston is route F 32. Along that drive are a number of Kirtland's Warbler viewing areas. Then there are those elk. A half hour north is Atlanta, known as the Elk Capital. You may not have to go that far. Elk are spotted in the forests just outside Lewiston all the time. It isn't out of the question to walk right up onto them, if you are quiet, while hiking or hunting morel mushrooms.

MANISTIQUE

IS

A

PLACE

WHERE

THEY

REALLY

DO

WALK

THE

WALK

MANISTIQUE GETAWAY

Manistique has always fascinated visitors, sportsmen, and explorers. Some young people were asking me where to go around the town. They had seen an online video about Kitch-iti-kipi, the Big Spring. They planned to go to the spring, but didn't know anything about the area. The video suggested finding an old-timer who might know some of the history and legends around Manistique. For some reason these kids came to me, as if I would know an old-timer, wanting to know how to find the attractions, where to eat, where to shop, and where to stay in case they were having that much fun. So, here we go.

The historic architecture, nature trails and waterways will have visitors walking all over the place. A few places to put on the list are the winery, Treasure City, , the largest gift shop in the upper peninsula. Plan to be there a while, there are 10,000 square feet of goodies to check out. Trader Bob's is another favorite out on Trader's Point. They are right across from the Upper Crust Cafe. The road to Trader's Point is the way to the kayak and canoe launch. Not as famous is a spot that is downtown, Tap 21 is a place with a collection of craft beers, vintage tin ceilings, and an 1893 Brunswick mahogany bar from Chicago. This is a place I never miss, because of their burger. I test burgers everywhere and will tell you that the Tap 21 Burger is one of the top 3 burgers in Michigan. I don't know what they do to it, but can tell you that my mouth is watering just writing about it.

As soon as you arrive, the bright red lighthouse, out in the sparkling water, will catch your eye. There will be signs describing the beaches, beautiful, and the boardwalk. Construction on the Manistique Boardwalk began in the early 1990s, with several extensions and improvements, in the intervening years. The boardwalk now runs almost 2 miles. Beginning at the eastern city limits, it offers breathtaking views of Lake Michigan, and that distinctive red lighthouse. Then it passes under the U. S. Highway 2 bridge, and heads into the downtown district. Along the way users can pause at a fishing pier, walk out to the east breakwater lighthouse, and rest up at the picnic grounds.

The Big Spring is always high on the list for a day trip to Manistique. Kitch-Iti-Kipi (cold big water), or The Big Spring, was a sacred place to the native inhabitants of this area. One of the names they gave it was the "Mirror of Heaven. Kitch-Iti-Kipi is the largest spring in Michigan, at 300 feet by 175 feet. Fed by more than 20 springs, it is refreshed continuously, with crystal-clear water. More than 10,000 gallons a minute gush up, from the limestone bed. There are several legends associated with the 40+ foot deep pool. One is, that in the past, some of the springs would spout columns of water high into the air. Another legend may explain the pattern at the bottom of the spring that, some say, resembles a beautiful Native American maiden. While her lover was absent, she was trying to elude an unwanted suitor, and dove into the spring. The magical qualities of the waters transformed her into a white deer. From this event came the taboo, among native tribes, against the killing of white deer. There are other legends, including the idea that the waters were lethal, since they don't freeze in winter, and no frogs or turtles live in the pool. The "Big Spring" is located just west of Manistique, at Palms Book State Park. Go downtown, then go across the river where the old siphon bridge is, and follow the signs. Alternately, go west of Manistique on U.S. 2 to Thompson, take M-149 north for 12 miles to the park. There is plenty of parking, and it is a short walk to the spring, along a paved path. A self-operated observation raft takes visitors across the spring, so you can view the underwater features. There is a State Park fee.

While on the subject of nature areas, Rainey Wildlife Area encompasses more than 100 acres of hardwood and conifer forests. A hiking trail passes through mixed hardwoods and conifers. There are boardwalks for the wet areas, and eventually you reach an elevated platform, that is excellent for bird-watching. The platform has a barrier-free ramp, that reaches mid-level, and offers a scenic view of the sedge meadow and open water wetlands. The trail crosses Smith Creek, which flows through a patterned fen, to Indian Lake. This area is popular for bird-watching. Warblers are found here, and it is not difficult to find nesting eagles. Be sure to bring your camera during fall color tour season. To get there from U.S. 2 in Manistique, drive north through town on M-94, about 5 miles, to Dawson Road. Turn left (west), and proceed 1.5 miles to an access road, that goes north to the site parking lot. There are no facilities at this area, so be prepared for spending some time in a fairly remote wilderness.

If you decide to visit Manistique in the winter, you won't go wrong. They have a Sno-Fest, ice fishing contests, and cross-country skiing. Just out of town to the west, the Indian Lake Pathways Ski Trail has trails ranging from just under a mile in length, to twenty three miles. The Rainey Wildlife Area is considered one of the best for snowshoeing. There are hundreds of miles of groomed trails leading off in every direction regardless of where you start. The "Thunder Bowl" has become a "must visit" playground for snowmobiles. It is the site of an abandoned ski hill, and attracts traditional sledders, as well as snowmobiles. The "Thunder Bowl" is 22 miles northwest of Manistique on Thunder Lake.

There is something else rare and wonderful here, the site of the old Siphon Bridge. It is hard to miss the Water Tower Museum and Siphon Bridge, where the historical society has been so effective. The tower, with a capacity of 200,000 gallons, is 200 feet tall in an octagon shape. The upper peninsula has seen a long list of engineering marvels, created during the lumber and mining booms, of previous centuries. One that is unique, perhaps in the world, was the Siphon Bridge in Manistique. In the early 1900s, the Manistique Pulp and Paper Company, had overcome tremendous obstacles to harness the power of the Manistique River for their manufacturing facility. Their efforts had included building a reinforced dam, a mill, and a canal, to confine the river. The canal is over 1/2 mile long, with concrete walls, rising above the river. While the canal worked perfectly, to deliver 650,000 gallons of water per hour to the mill wheel, the height of the sides made it nearly impossible, to raise bridges across the canal. The fantastic solution was the Siphon Bridge.

The Siphon Bridge was built in 1919. The roadway itself, was as much as 4 feet BELOW the water level. The bridge was supported by water, that was forced under it, using atmospheric pressure. The feed flume was 3,000 feet long and 200 feet wide. The engineering is amazing. This whole project was about like carrying the bridge across the river, in a half-cylinder, set in the water of the canal. Full sets of plans and demonstrations are available at the museum. In its original form, the bridge was listed in "Ripley's Believe It or Not", because the road was actually below the level of the water in the flume.

There is a lot more around town so visitors often decide to extend their stay. The Visitors Center, with the statue of Paul Bunyan, is right on Highway 2. They have all the maps and the contact information for the lodging and attractions.

OLD TOWN

HAS

BECOME

THE

PREMIER

ARTS

DESTINATION

IN

THE

CAPITAL

OF

MICHIGAN

OLD TOWN GETAWAY

Old Town is one of those historic district restorations we hear about on the news. It also happens to be one that succeeded beyond anyone's aspirations. Simply put in the Lansing area, when something new is going to happen, when a new festival is going to start up, when a creative person looks at mid-Michigan, these days, that person or group is going to take a good look at Old Town. Some of us watched in amazement as Old Town became a destination. We, who grew up in the 1960s, remember the decline of the area referred to in those days a the "north side". It was always a rough area and became rougher each year. Some people wouldn't even go there. Now, it is the premier destination in the capitol city.

A few dedicated people decided that the decay of the "north side"must stop. Among these visionaries were the late Robert Busby, photographer Richard Galosy and an entrepreneur, Kathy Holcomb, who believed in Old Town early on, put her talent on the line, and opened the Absolute Gallery. In 1996, the Mainstreet program was established in Old Town. Since then, crime rates have fallen to the lowest in the city, building vacancy has dropped from 90 percent to less than 10 percent, and Old Town is proud to be home to some of the finest art and entertainment venues in mid-Michigan. Old Town has been become a favorite destination and, if you go on a weekend, there is very likely to be a festival going on. It's hard to believe that this was once known as the "north side" and was as rough a neighborhood and you could find. Now it is on a lot of "urban hiking" lists.

Old Town has become the arts destination in central Michigan. To find out what is happening in the arts scene stop in at the Absolute Gallery on Grand River just east of Turner Road. No only is the gallery packed with the work of local artists and artisans, the owners will be there and they know all about Old Town. Their mission is to "facilitate the appreciation of art in our community, the growth of our artists, and innovative programming." The gallery craft boutique is a shopper's paradise of gifts and uncommon accessories for the home, office and special items suitable for children. The variety is the result of their unrelenting search for quality goods from local, regional, and national sources. It all adds up to shopping experience like none other in the city.

Along with all the shops, galleries, and eateries there are a couple of distinct localities to visit. One is the Brenke Fish Ladder, on the Grand River, which was built in 1981. It was constructed so fish could get around the dam as they head upstream. The fish ladder is a popular place to pause along the Lansing River Trail. There are almost always fishermen nearby, catching catfish, carp, sunfish, and other smaller species. In early autumn this is an excellent place for spotting salmon. Fishing within the ladder is not permitted.

Another distinctive destination, the Dodge Mansion, is

also known as Turner-Dodge House. Built in 1855, the Turner-Dodge House is now a museum, preserving the history of Lansing's early pioneers. The style is Classical Revival and this is the only 19th century residence in the region that is open to the public. The mansion is located at 100 East North Street and is open all year Tuesday – Friday.

Old Town has become well known for innovative eateries. One that is as distinctive as this whole district is Golden Harvest, at 1625 Turner St. The food here is amazing at this tiny breakfast/brunch stop. The portions are generous to say the least. What you need to plan for is the wait. The restaurant is small and so popular that there is almost always a wait and, the wait is outdoors because there is no indoor waiting room. Everything they serve is an innovation. My advice is live a little and order something different from your usual. You can't go wrong just ordering the specials. The pace is hectic, but the staff are pros so it is all part of a fun time.

There is something else rare and wonderful here. The architecture is historic and some of these old buildings are said to be haunted. So many are instances of spectral activity have been reported that the community has developed the Old Town Ghost Tour. If interested in details, head over to the Absolute Gallery again, the owners swear it is totally haunted. Kathy tells it this way. "When I came into this business, I didn't believe in ghosts. But I know how gravity works". She goes on to describe the day she saw a picture move sideways across her store's wall instead of falling straight down. She has also had price tags mysteriously go missing from her inventory. She says two ghosts live in the gallery: a man named George and a small child, who were both involved in a train accident. Ghosts or no ghosts, a day spent in Old Town will be a lot of fun.

OTHER GREAT LAKES GETAWAY

Up in Northern Michigan lies Roscommon County. In that county are Michigan's other "Great Lakes"; a wonderland of natural beauty that is hard to beat. This is the heart of the state, so the "Other Great Lakes" are just a short drive from most anywhere in Michigan. This region has acres of forests, nature areas, old growth pines, miles of trails, and those fantastic lakes. The other "Great Lakes" are Houghton, Higgins, and Lake St. Helen. All three lakes will delight you with their natural beauty, wildlife viewing, and spectacular sunrises and sunsets. The combination of the three makes this region a sportsman's fishing and boating paradise. Here is a bit about each of those lakes.

Houghton Lake is Michigan's largest inland lake. It is more than 7 miles long and more than 4 miles wide. For its size this is a fairly shallow lake, averaging just under 8 feet in depth. The south end of the lake has the most development. Prudenville is where you find lodging, restaurants and shopping. Houghton Lake is the site of one of a traditional winter event, Tip-Up-Town. Back in 1951, a couple of the guys were trying to figure out how to pass the long winter months on Houghton Lake. They decided to have a festival. A nationwide contest was held to come up with a name for the event. They eventually settled on Tip-Up-Town USA, a reference to the little flag on an ice fishing rig that signals a bite. Today, the festival is huge, requiring more than 200 volunteers.

Events, like sled dogs, polar dip, medallion hunt, and dozens of contests and parades are held in January.

Directly north of Houghton Lake, and 5 miles west of Roscommon, is Higgins Lake. Higgins was formed when the glacier retreated north. This lake has been written of as one of the world's most beautiful lakes. Even in prehistory, the beauty of this lake was noted. The Chippewa people called the lake Majinabeesh, which means "sparkling water". The crystal clear lake is connected to Marl Lake by the Cut River. That means that there are fish, especially perch, trout and pike. Two state parks and public access points provide excellent beach facilities and boat launches.

A few miles east of Houghton and Higgins is Lake St. Helen. The lake is about 2,400 acres, very shallow, except for a couple holes, and is full of fish. Due to the differences in depth, different species of fish are found in different places on the water. The lake is man-made and seems to be three different lakes, known locally as, 1st lake, 2nd lake, and 3rd lake. One side of the lake is almost entirely free of development. It is under lease to the Duck Club. The community of St. Helen is all about outdoor activities. In fact, signs at the edge of town call this a "recreational community".

A getaway to the "Other Great Lakes" can be more than just the water. There are scenic drives, old growth pines, historical monuments, and unique attractions to explore.

Three different drives will take visitors to three areas that are distinct from each other. Old Highway 27, runs north and south, just west of the lakes. The Houghton Lake Flats is a wildlife restoration project, designed to provide habitat for waterfowl and other wetland species. An observation deck, and handicapped accessible gazebo, provide visitors with a place to stop and enjoy the wide variety of birds that now populate the flats. This drive will also take you to the spot where all those Osprey's are nesting. The Roscommon County Quilt Trail, is another fun and interesting way, to explore this beautiful part of Michigan. Families in this area, have preserved and handed down, traditional family quilts through generations. Now these patterns are displayed on buildings and barns throughout the County. Many of the quilt patterns tell stories about family history and cultures. About 10 miles north of Prudenville is Lansing Road. The gravel section, between M-18 and County Road 100, has been designated a Natural Beauty Road. The road runs through a stand of White Birch trees believed to be the largest tract left in lower Michigan. It is gravel, but it is beautiful.

As one drives around, way-signing identifies some of the fun local attractions and historical monuments. At the Fireman's Memorial, a bronze firefighter standing twelve feet tall and weighing around 2,000 pounds, is the centerpiece of the site. The statue was created by Michigan craftsman Edward Chesney. The grounds include picnic and play areas. If you visit this memorial on a weekday, like I did, you may find that you are the only person there. Wandering the grounds, and studying the names of the fallen, is an emotional experience. This memorial is dedicated to the members of that unselfish organization of men and women, who hold devotion to duty above personal risk, protecting the lives, homes, and property of their fellow citizens, from the ravages of fire and other disasters. Each year, usually during the 3rd week of September, a festival is held in remembrance these brave citizens. During the event there is a parade, antique equipment demonstration, a memorial service, a light parade, music, dancing, and emergency crew competitions. The Firemen's Memorial is just south of Roscommon about 1/2 mile east of M-18.

The Historical Village, on the south end of Houghton Lake, is one of the most extensive in Michigan. There are 11 restored buildings from the 1800s to visit on the self-guided tour, including a schoolroom, Blue Star Museum, town hall, dress shop, general store, doctor's office/ pharmacy, barber shop, a homestead, a chapel and others. The schoolhouse is an original hand-hewn log structure, built in 1876 to serve the children of Edna, now named Prudenville. The Village Days festival brings the village to life, through demonstrations, and guides in period costumes. All of the buildings are open for the event, and are operating just as they would have, when originally built. The event also includes craft and musical demonstrations.

The Civilian Conservation Corps was formed to "put Americans back to work". Over 100,000 of Michigan's young men journeyed to CCC Camps all over the state, to work on reforestation and conservation projects. Between 1933 and 1942, these workers planted more than 480 million trees, constructed 7,000 miles of truck trails, 504 bridges, and 222 buildings. The CCC (Civilian Conservation Corps) Museum, exhibits photographs and artifacts to paint the picture of the CCC workers day-to-day life and accomplishments. The grounds are across from North Higgins Lake State Park, on North Higgins Lake Drive, and include a replica CCC barracks building with exhibits.

Some of the attractions are different from most any you will find in other parts of Michigan. In the northern part of Roscommon County, is an area with sandy soils and small grassy openings, scattered throughout the forest of young jack pine trees. These conditions, are the unique habitat, that is required for the endangered Kirtland's Warbler to nest and breed. There are only about 3,000 of these birds left, and they return to Jack Pines of Roscommon County, every year. On West Rose City Road, north of St. Helen, is the Ogemaw Nature Park. This is a cool place to take the kids. Older deer that have been rescued are in the park and visitors can feed them. One popular feature is the albino deer that live at the park. There are also fawns, goats, and a pig or two. The park has a picnic area, and has food available to feed to the animals. The park is usually open from noon to 7:00

pm. The Lost Twin Lakes Pathway, has features that few other local trails can match. This trail has remained relatively unknown due to its remote location off a gravel road. The trail is in part of the Au Sable State Forest. The loop runs a bit over 3 miles, and became an Eagle Scout project a few years ago. They built a number of bridges and boardwalks over the wettest parts of the trail. If you are looking for a pleasant walk in the woods, this is the pathway for you. There are century-old white pines that survived the lumbering days. Some of these pines are as much as five feet around. In addition, there are ridges, sinkholes, wetlands, and swamps along with those small lakes, from which the pathway gets its name. Lost Twin Lakes is open to Nordic skiing and snowshoeing as well as mountain biking.

There is something else rare and wonderful here, an old growth forest. The Red Pines Nature Area is a DNR project. This 34-acre grove of virgin red pine, is one of the best stands left in the mid-west portion of the United States. It is an excellent example of the virgin pine forest, that once covered this part of Michigan. At one time, this grove of old-growth red pines and jack pines, was home to the largest red pine in Michigan, a former National Champion red pine. That old champion pine is no longer living, but there are several gigantic members of the species, still standing in this forest. The pathway threads its way through fairly flat terrain, in a natural area, that has not been altered by the hand of man, since European explorers rediscovered it. As you walk through the stand, there are points where you are completely surrounded by giant trees. When you reach the center point of the grove, it is easy to imagine that you have traveled to the past, back to the time when the great forests covered all of Northern Michigan. There is evidence of the great fires that swept through in 1798, 1888, and 1928, yet, the towering pines remain.

Should you decide to stay over, there is affordable lodging of every kind around the lakes. When you arrive you will find lodging options from luxurious waterfront hotels and family-owned motels to quaint cottages and rustic cabins, or choose to camp at private and state park campgrounds. There are casual and fine dining establishments, amusement parks, state parks, theaters, trails, and beaches. Not to mention those glorious stars at night in the clear dark skies.

THE

ROCHESTER HILLS

MUSEUM

AT

VAN HOOSEN

FARM

IS

ONE

OF

THE

BEST

IN

MICHIGAN

ROCHESTER AREA GETAWAY

A getaway to Rochester Hills, and the Greater Rochester Area, will be a surprise to travelers who are unfamiliar with the metropolitan Detroit area. A beautiful community thrives amid the hustle and bustle of an urban environment. Busy, busy was my first impression of this city within a city, so busy. Then I began to discover the gems and treasures hidden away. There are trails and nature areas, shops and dining, and great places for the kids to play. Then there are the incredible historic destinations and architecture that is unmatched in most of America, let alone Michigan.

There are two principle shopping and dining districts in the area, downtown Rochester and the Villages of Rochester Hills. Each is distinct from the other and will add to the fun of a quick getaway. Downtown Rochester shopping is mostly on the main thoroughfare. Shops include well known names and the completely unique. You can find western gear, a soap factory and unique independent boutiques like Simply The Best. Simply The Best is kind of hidden, but worth seeking out. They work hard to bring the latest trends and fashions, season to season. The Villages of Rochester Hills is described as a 375,000 square foot shopping and dining district. The first in Michigan to embrace a streetscape concept. The variety of merchants is amazing and the venue is beautiful with a fountain, gazebo, and a small park. Visitors will find national and local retailers in along tree-lined boulevards with on-street parking.

The dining options are just as varied. Across this region can be found every imaginable type of eatery, from delis to cider mills to fine dining. I have sampled several and can recommend three that I will return to again and again. Kruse and Muer is a spot where you can have a casual lunch or take in an ambiance suitable for an anniversary celebration. The food is scrumptious. O'Connor's Public House is an Irish pub that knows how to build a Guinness. Further, they can cook. They have excellent Scotch Eggs and I will order the Irish Ham & Cabbage again, next time I am there. Then there is the Home Bakery located in the oldest commercial building in town. They have created a confection that is a combination of a croissant and a donut, called the Kronut. I am no expert on pastry, but this is the most delicious I have ever tasted. When you get your first one, be sure to take a great big deep first bite, just nothing like it. There are more dining places I have yet to try, can't wait. Between, and around, these two shopping/dining districts are nature areas, historic destinations and unusual attractions.

One of the major attractions in the region is the Rochester Hills Museum at Van Hoosen Farm. This complex of buildings, gardens, and exhibits preserves the lives and legacy of some of the most remarkable women in the history of Michigan. They were part of a pioneer family who shaped this region and the wider world. Dr. Bertha

Van Hoosen, Alice Van Hoosen Jones, and Dr. Sarah Van Hoosen Jones traveled the world. Those journeys were instrumental in the education of all three. These women broke through a number of social barriers in pursuit of their achievements. The history their groundbreaking activities can be relived by a visit to the Van Hoosen Farm. Stoney Creek runs along one border of the farm. The creek was important; several mills operated on it and it lent its name to the entire area for a time. The Stoney Creek Schoolhouse building is a living history classroom.

The main residence contains the history and the artifacts of the Taylor and Van Hoosen families. Inside, items brought by the first Taylor and Van Hoosen family members, can be seen and appreciated. There are furnishings from five generations, including candelabras from Italy, a Medici tapestry, and all manner of furnishings from their travels in Europe and the Orient. The home includes some unusual construction features like the bread warmer built into the brickwork of the fireplace. Then there is the absence of shower heads in the baths. At one time it was believed that the pulsing of a shower would damage a woman's delicate skin.

There are more structures to explore at the farm like, the Red House. There are several exhibits showing farm life and the implements required in those days. The museum complex is surrounded by sixteen acres of park grounds. There are huge old walnut and maple trees, and acres of flowers. It all makes for a beautiful place to wander, take pictures and nap beneath the clear blue skies. The Museum buildings and grounds are owned and operated by the City of Rochester Hills, as part of the Rochester Hills Parks Department. The Rochester Garden Club maintains the gardens. Guided tours of this fascinating building are available on Fridays and Saturdays. Other times are available by appointment. The Van Hoosen Farmhouse is listed on the National Register of Historic Places. This quick and easy getaway is sponsored by the Rochester Hills Museum at Van Hoosen Farm.

The entire Rochester region welcomes nature lovers. Trails cross the town and connect the parks. At eight feet wide, The Paint Creek Trail is roomy for hiking, biking, horse back riding, and other non-motorized activities. The trail is pet friendly. It runs through Rochester Hills into Rochester where it intersects with the River Walk Trail, which connects to the Clinton River Trail. The Clinton River Trail runs across Oakland County into Rochester. It is part of the Great Lake to Lake Trail which will connect Port Huron to South Haven. While all of the nature areas are cool, Bloomer Park has some unusual features and an unusual history. The park is just one of 15 established by Howard Bloomer, who is considered the father of Michigan's State Park and Huron Clinton Metropark systems. Bloomer Park has trails and recreation facilities. There is a steep hill, about 175 feet, that was the site of a ski jump known as Newberry Hill. In the 1920s Newberry Hill was the largest ski jump in the lower peninsula. Currently there is a large stone building on that spot that was built as part of the CCC program. There is another fun venue in this park, the first Velodrome in Michigan was constructed here. If you haven't seen one, it is a big oval with banked sides that is for high speed bicycle racing.

Many people make the trip to this area for the festivals. There is something going on all the time. In summer there are the Garden Walk, Festival of the Hills, and Fine Art at the Village. The Stone Wall Pumpkin Festival is part of the October celebrations at Van Hoosen Farm. Thousands of people show up to take part in the pumpkin carving, pumpkin bowling, and general mayhem. When the carving is finished, as many as 1,000 pumpkins are perched on the historic stone walls surrounding the museum. Then each of the pumpkins is lit up and the night comes alive. This coordinates with the Scarecrows in the City event. The Big Bright Light Show usually begins just before Thanksgiving and runs through January 1st. This festival involves covering the shopping district of downtown Rochester with over 1,000,000 bulbs. Several companion events go on during the 5 week festival, including Lagniappe, and free horse-drawn carriage rides in the early evening.

There is something else rare and wonderful here, Meadow Brook Hall. For the first half hour after you enter the grounds of Meadow Brook Hall, your vocabulary may well be reduced to two expressions, ooooh and aaaah! No matter how many magnificent buildings one has seen, this place will remain in the memory as a truly impressive creation. It takes a while to wander the grounds and gardens. A tour of the inside is amazing. The woodwork alone can overwhelm the senses. Even the exterior chimneys are works of art. An easy stroll through the extensive gardens is a great way to see the mansion from several different perspectives. Special events include a Holiday Walk and the Holiday Walk Tours of the mansion.

Meadow Brook was the estate of Matilda and John F. Dodge. After John passed, Matilda wed Alfred Wilson, a lumber baron. A written description is not like an actual visit, but here are a few statistics just the same. The manor has 110 rooms within 88,000 square feet. There are 24 fireplaces served by those unique brick chimneys, of which, there are 39 up on the roof. Then there is the secret passage. You can't have a "castle" without secret passageways. There is one, it is a staircase from Alfred's game room to his office upstairs. There is even a beauty parlor that was built for the lady of the house.

The dining room ceiling is a sculpture, the woodwork throughout is the best. There are Tiffany stained glass windows, custom-made hardware and 75,000 pieces of art, furniture, ceramics and more throughout. If that weren't enough, the mansion sits on an estate comprised of more than 1,400 acres. There are lawns, fountains, a gazebo and beautiful sculptures. The children, Frances and Daniel, had playhouses hidden away in woods.

Meadow Brook Hall is regarded as the finest example of Tudor-revival architecture in America. It is the sixth largest historic house in the United States and the third largest in Michigan. The Hall was designated a National Historic Landmark in 2012.

SALINE

HAS

BEEN

VOTED

IN THE

TOP

100

PLACES

IN

AMERICA

TO

LIVE

SALINE GETAWAY

A day trip getaway to Saline could end up becoming a longer stay. There still exists a town where the shop and restaurant owners know your name. Where kids feel safe to play, the schools are exceptional, families love to stroll, and where old time conveniences are close by. Saline is a place where things are a little slower, a little simpler, and just a little quieter. A charming downtown, beautiful parks and trails and a rich history are some of the elements that contribute to the environment that makes Saline, Michigan so special. In 2012 Bloomberg Businessweek named Saline the "Best Place to Raise Kids" in Michigan. Saline has been voted the best place to raise kids, because the quality of life remains in the top tier in Michigan. Three times, (2005, 2007, and 2009) Saline has been honored by CNN/Money Magazine as one of the "Top 100 Best Places to Live" in the United States. That list is the result of extensive research in areas like financial performance, housing, education, quality of life, leisure and culture, and healthcare facilities.

Not only is Saline a great place to live, it is a fun place to visit. The downtown district has all kinds of cool places to shop and an eclectic group of dining options. Within just a few blocks there is Benny's Bakery, Smokehouse 52, Sweet Lelani's Deserts and The Cheese Shop. The Stone Lake Brewery and Salt Springs Brewery are perfecting craft beers. Sprinkled in between the dining spots are a whole range of unique shops to explore. In one shopping center, is one of just a few Emagine theaters found in Michigan. This is a new way to experience "going to the movies". Amenities include gourmet concessions, power recliners or DBOX Motion seats, and valet parking. Some say this is the only way to go these days.

Festivals and events draw people to Saline throughout the year. There is the Farmer's Market, Ladies Night Out, Sports Cars to Saline, the Saline Summerfest, the Harvest of the Arts, Mastodon Obstacle Run, Oktoberfest, Summer Music Series, and Taste of Saline. Saline has a Celtic Festival that is second to none and a holiday craft show that has been voted the best in Michigan.

Situated as it is, on the Great Sauk Trail, Saline is a special place when it comes to Michigan history. U.S. 12 was the main traffic artery between the terminus of the Erie Canal and Chicago, the gateway to the west. Settlers, pioneers, and adventurers made their way along this highway. Among the destinations of note on the "Trail" is the Rentschler Farm Museum, located on the east end of town. The museum occupies four acres of land and consists of a frame house and eleven outbuildings. The architecture of the house was borrowed from several styles, but is dominated by the Queen Anne fish scale accent in the gable and a wrap-around gingerbread porch. The outbuildings consist of a restored workshop, hog house, an original 19th century shed, large equipment barn, hen house, corn crib, upper and lower barns, a sheep barn, small equipment shed, an ice house and a windmill. The museum is the site of a major holiday event in December.

The Depot Museum is on The Depot Trail, a rails to trails conversion that runs between North Ann Arbor and Harris Streets in downtown. This is one of the best examples of a rail to trail project. The surface is a combination of crushed limestone and asphalt to provide a surface that is great for biking, walking and running. The trail is 8–10 feet wide so there is room for walkers, wheelchairs, bikes and in-line skaters. Along the way are plantings, benches and some great artwork.

One historic structure that always catches the eye is the Davenport-Curtiss mansion, built in 1876. The house and grounds take up an impressive chunk of land right on Michigan Avenue. The house is so impressive that many travelers assumed it must be a public building; it is actually a private residence. The Curtiss family still has the blueprints, written on linen, called for a Second Empire design with a tower and mansard roof. The plans called for the use of only the finest materials available. As an example, the bathtubs were solid walnut with copper linings. Those were removed during one renovation. The grounds contain a matching carriage house and stable. The landscaping included trees rarely found in Michigan.

There is something else rare and wonderful here, the Bixby Marionettes. Almost unknown to the youth of today, these remarkable hand-carved puppets entertained children and adults with shows like Alladin, The Wizard of Oz, and The Magic Stalk. Meredith Bixby and his wife, Thyra, began carving the jointed bodies of the puppets at home. They produced the costumes, staging, lighting, scripts and scenery. The Meredith Marionettes Touring Company staged shows all across the country in schools, theaters, and community centers. For decades before the advent of the digital age, children waited eagerly for the next show where animals talked, peasant huts could walk, and good always overcame evil. Every summer the Bixby crew would prepare a new show and open the season by staging it at their studio in Saline. The local kids were the first ones to see the show that would be seen in person by a quarter of a million other children each year. The collection is on display at the District Library on Maple Road. Unfortunately, available space is limited so the collection is shown in small parts on a rotating basis. Even so, when you see these puppets, you can almost hear the sounds of the wicked magician as he begins to weave his evil plot.

TAWAS BAY GETAWAY

Get to trading stories about beaches around Michigan and the conversation is probably going to dwell on the beaches and dunes along Lake Michigan. Another of the secrets about the Sunrise Side, is that there are beautiful unspoiled beaches at Tawas Bay. Six different beaches provide miles of golden sand. In addition, there are biking and hiking trails, and extensive woodlands, that make Tawas Bay a great getaway. The bay is defined by a curved point of land. On the southern end is Tawas City Shoreline Park and on the other end of the curve is Tawas Point State Park and the Tawas Point Lighthouse. Those two points are connected by good roads, biking and walking trails and those beautiful beaches. Tawas Bay is perfect for sailing, paddling, fishing, power boating, and wave runners. It is also a favorite destination for kite boarding. All of the Lake Huron beaches slope gently down to the bay, creating a great place for outings to play in the sand and water.

There are attractions all around the Bay. The principal shopping district, Newman Street, has a range of shopping and dining options that can keep one busy all day. If you are looking for gifts or just want to enjoy a unique shopping destination, Newman Street is the place to go. In just a few blocks, with plenty of parking, you'll find everything from chocolate to jewelry to local art. The Tawas Bay Art Council & Gallery, also on Newman St. promotes the work of local artists for the benefit and enjoyment of the community. If you miss the good old days, and those great variety stores, head over to Mooney's Ben Franklin. Mooney's, at 138 Newman St. in East Tawas, was established as a family business in 1944, and it is still run as a family business today. Here is the short list of what you'll find souvenirs, games, beach stuff, camping goodies, puzzles, tons of indoor and outdoor activities, clothes, hardware, crafts, knitting, quilting, home cottage cabin camper decor, garden decor, cards, sunglasses. The people who run Mooney's are always friendly and helpful, if you can't find it, just ask. They probably have it somewhere in the store.

There are other attractions to see on a day trip. The Tawas Point Lighthouse is just a short ride from downtown. Tawas Point is a favorite spot for watching migratory birds. It is particularly well-known for the varieties of warblers that gather there. Over 160 species were recorded during the Birding Festival weekend in 2016. Other festivals in the area include Perchville, which is one of the longest running festivals in Northern Michigan, and the Tawas Point Lighthouse Festival. Another spot for bird watching is the Eagle's Nest Overlook at the Canoe Memorial. The nest has been used by a pair of bald eagles since the 1980s. If you head out there, binoculars will come in handy.

The golden beaches of Tawas Bay include; Tawas City Beach on U.S. 23 has grills, picnic areas, changing areas, restrooms & day fee. Tawas Point State Park on Tawas

Beach Rd. has all facilities & fee. Sand Lake Beach on Indian Lake Rd. a U.S Forest Service Fee area, picnic area, pit toilet. Long Lake Public Beach on Kokosing Rd in Hale has picnic, swimming and beach & no fee. Loon Lake Public Beach west of Hale to Putnam Rd. has picnic area, pit toilet & no fee.

Inland from the beaches is the Huron National Forest. The Au Sable River is a major attraction and the trails through the forest are some of the best in Michigan. The Corsair Trails System is the crown jewel of the Silver Valley. There are many miles of scenic groomed trails for hiking and cross country skiing. The lure is the forest itself, the deep snowfalls, and the clean fresh air. There are amazing scenic views from such spots as Silver Valley and the high banks. At the Au Sable Highbanks, you can see clear across the Au Sable River Valley. Sometimes you can watch thunder heads and snowstorms advancing from 20 miles away. The Hoist Lakes Trail System will offer a challenge for even the expert adventure skier. There are 10,000 acres and over 20 miles of excellent trails.

There is something else rare and wonderful here. Legend says that the wreck of the long lost Griffin, the first boat to sail the Great Lakes, is nearby. In the 17th century, the French explorer LaSalle sailed north on the Griffin. On the homeward leg of the journey, the Griffin went missing somewhere on Lake Huron. The ship was never found. The earliest settlers in the Tawas Bay region discovered the remnants of a ship rotting away in the sand at Lake Solitude a half mile inland from Lake Huron. While the ship skeleton was certainly a mystery, the battle for survival in those days meant there was little time for investigation, but the story of the wreck lived on in tales told around night fires through the long winters. Some say that it can't be the Griffin, too far inland, but there is evidence that Lake Solitude was actually part of Lake Huron back in those days. Accurate maps just don't exist from that time. Could the Griffin have been seeking shelter from one of those legendary Lake Huron storms? Did the storm drive them aground and wreck them in the remote wilderness? The debate goes on. A visit to Iosco County Historical Museum might be worth the effort.

THREE WATERFALLS GETAWAY

This quick and easy getaway is a day trip to three different waterfalls. Bond falls is the largest and most famous. The other two are Agate Falls and Canyon Falls.

Bond Falls is one of the most popular and beautiful waterfalls in the upper peninsula of Michigan. It also happens to be one of the easiest to visit. The waterfall is on the middle branch of the Ontonagon River, a few miles east of Route 45 on Bond Falls Road. The entrance is a gravel road, that winds downhill to the parking area, immediately adjacent to the trails and walks along the waterfall. The waterfall drops about 50 feet and there is a boardwalk that extends across the river, below the base of the falls, where one can get a perfect view. There are trails on both sides of the waterfall that afford different points of view and photo opportunities. The old trail, with some steep rocky climbs on the east side of the falls, is still accessible for hikers and there are other trails through the woods.

Bond Falls is beautiful, and popular, in all seasons, summer and fall being the busiest. In winter, snowmobile riders can drive right down to the parking area, but cars are best left at the top near the gate. It is just a short walk down to the falls. The river continues its drop of nearly 900 feet en route to Lake Superior. To the north the river drops again, at Agate Falls.

Located on Route 28, Agate Falls is an entirely different experience, and can be reached by continuing on Bond Falls Road. There is good parking near the falls, with walking trails leading along the river. In the warm months this is a favorite spot to stop, picnic, and enjoy the roaring river. The trail along the river makes it possible to hike down below the waterfall for great picture taking opportunities. One unique feature of this waterfall location is the old rail road bridge that crosses the river. That bridge is now part of a rail to trails project and is a popular snowmobile route in winter. It may not be easy to get up there, but I can tell you that it is worth it. Especially in the winter time, the views from the old railroad trestle are breathtaking.

Canyon Falls is a short drive away. Continue east on Route 28 to the intersection with Route 41. Head north toward L'Anse and Alberta. Just south of Alberta is the park entrance to reach Canyon Falls. Canyon Falls, is a box canyon waterfall and sometimes called the Grand Canyon of the Upper Peninsula. In the summer months the hike along the boardwalk follows the course of the Sturgeon River to the waterfall. There are actually several drops that comprise the falls. At the far end is the payoff. The furthest waterfall roars and plunges through a canyon and is a contender for best waterfall in the upper peninsula. In the winter months the parking area is closed, but you can park at the pull off, then snowshoe into the falls. If you go in winter, you may well have the whole wilderness to yourself. The silence of the forest is broken only by the sound of the river rushing down the canyon and the occasional bird song. Parts of the river may be frozen and the water will come ripping out of the ice dam on the downstream side. This is a winter hike that can be cold and wet, but the scenery makes it worth every bit of it. It is so beautiful, we wondered why we were the only people there.

There are a lot of other destinations to discover in the forests around Paulding. If you feel like another waterfall, O Kun De Kun Falls is just to the north of Paulding. It does involve a hike along a fairly rough trail. That trail will intersect with the North Country Trail at the falls. O Kun De Kun is a plunge falls and, when it is in full flow, you can actually walk behind the waterfall.

If you want to go out at night, Paulding is the place where the Paulding Ghost Light has been spotted for a couple of generations now. The best place to see the "ghost light" is just south of Paulding. These days it is usually reported from the dead end on Robbins Rd. If you plan to stay in the area, the Running Bear Resort has excellent cabins and they know the entire area very well.

There is something else rare and wonderful here. This whole region has been a crossroads of travel since prehistory. The evidence is all around of this travel, often involving water. There are ancient constructions in remote locations, sometimes on islands. The watercraft display a remarkable level of skill and knowledge. A dugout canoe was discovered in 1953. The canoe was found at the the southern end of Thousand Island. The canoe was partially buried in the sand at the bottom of the lake. There was a small tree growing out of the end that was near the surface. It is made from a single white pine log. The craft is over 32 feet long, it is 31 inches wide at the center, the sides are 21 inches high. The walls of the canoe are 1 ½ inches thick. This canoe was large enough to transport 15-20 people. Archaeologists believe this dugout is native and one of the most significant found in Michigan. The presence of metal bars and oarlocks can be explained. It is thought that lumberjacks found this canoe and added the metal parts. The dugout was taken out of the lake in 1954 and is on display in the Lac Vieux Desert Casino.

TIP OF THE THUMB GETAWAY

The "thumb" of Michigan has sometimes been referred to as the "forgotten digit" of the mitten. Forgotten or not, there is a getaway at the tip that will be talked about long after you return home, no matter which part of it you jump into. For the fun of it, the "tip" runs roughly speaking from Port Hope in the east, to Bay Port in the west, with Grindstone City, Port Austin and Caseville in between. The whole area hugs the coast of Lake Huron. Visitors almost automatically begin to focus on Lake Huron. The waters are pure and blue, lighthouses are visible and legends of shipwrecks beckon. There are beaches, as well, so those who want nothing more than sunshine, sand and the sound of the waves are going to be happy too.

Coming up the Lake Huron shore, on Route 25 from the south, Port Hope is the first town on the "tip of the thumb". There are eleven designated sites in Port Hope on the National Register of Historic Places. The old chimney is the last one in existence from the lumbering era. It was part of the Stafford Lumber Mill Company. Port Hope is also a good place for those hunting the shipwrecks in the Thumb Area Bottomland Preserve. There are more than 20 major shipwrecks in the waters of the "tip of the thumb".

Heading north, Huron City is next a bit past the The Pointe Aux Barques lighthouse. Huron City is known for its museums based on historic buildings. There is a Life Saving Station, General Store, and others. The most distinctive is one known as the House of Seven Gables. In addition to those, tours include the rooming house, church, and a log cabin.

Further north is Grindstone City. As the name suggests, the town was of great importance in the grindstone industry. The abrasive stone quarried there was the finest found anywhere in the United States. The mill produced whet stones and scythe stones. The stones made here varied in size and weight from small kitchen stones weighing from 2 ½ to 10 lbs. and from 6 to 10 inches in diameter; to the huge grinding stones that weighed over two tons. The largest stone ever turned weighed over 6,600 lbs. It all ended when carborundum was developed after the First World War. The industry was discontinued about 1929. A memorial stone, on the corner of Copeland and Rouse Road, said to weigh 4,750 lbs.

At the northern most point of the thumb is Port Austin. This is the largest town on the getaway and could take up a whole day on its own. In town are shops, dining options of all kinds, including PAKS Backyard, a beer garden. Port Austin is one of the few places where you can watch the sun rise over a Great Lake and watch it set over a Great Lake. Port Crescent State Park on the beach has a five-mile long hiking trail, and there is the "Tip of the Thumb Heritage Water Trail" for kayakers and canoeists. If you plan to go out onto Lake Huron, Port Austin Kayak & Bike Rental is the place to get equipment, information about the Tip of The Thumb Heritage Water Trail, and that all important weather update. Just offshore is the Port Austin Lighthouse, which was occupied by a keeper until 1953, when it was automated. It is one and a half to two and a half miles from shore, depends on who you ask, off the tip of the Michigan "Thumb", resting on the reef that it marks. The water is as shallow as 3 feet in some places, and it is clear enough to see the dangerous rocks below. Divers can explore limestone ledges, walls and sunken islands along the Port Austin reef near the lighthouse. There are shipwrecks and even some grindstones lost from Grindstone City. For a gorgeous view of Lake Huron, stop in at Lisa's Loft in the historic brick building at the corner of Lake and Spring Streets above Heins Hardware. The view is truly breathtaking. Besides offering the view, Lisa's is a great shop with large selection of everyday gifts and seasonal items.

Continuing west travelers will find Caseville, famous for their Winter Fest in. I know of families who go every year just to join in the human bowling tournament. See, you lay on a sled of some sort and a loving family member propels you down the ice to collide with orange traffic barrels set up like bowling pins. Heading toward Caseville there is a very fine nature area called the

Wilderness Arboretum. Back in the day, local kids call it "The Woods", where they could explore dry forests and wetlands. The Arboretum is home to all manner of native Michigan plants and animals, birds and wildflowers protected by shallow wetlands, and sandy ridges extending to the nearby beach. This beautiful nature center, has a number of easy to walk, well maintained trails, including handicapped access trails. The wilderness arboretum encompasses over 100 acres of natural beauty, convenience facilities and a Visitor Center. The paved handicapped accessible trail is a walk into the giant oak trees and an amazing variety of wildflowers. The trail leads to one of the few dry swales found in this region, a forested ridge, and eventually, onto a boardwalk that leads to an interdunal wetland. The longer trails are mostly improved with wood chips, and will take hikers to that same dry swale and a wooded ridge habitat. These trails will also wind through moist woods and wetlands, as well as, stands of hardwoods. Boardwalks are provided in particularly wet areas. There are benches along the way where nature lovers can rest, or simply pause, to drink in the pure forest air.

Finally, to the west is Bay Port. This is a very small town, but it is worth the drive just for the fish at the Bay Port Fish Company. Fishermen, out of Bay Port, have been bringing in the bounty of Lake Huron since the early 1840s. These days, the Bay Port Fish Company continues the tradition. They have fresh and smoked fish available every day.

There is something else rare and wonderful here. Many visitors go to the "tip of the thumb" just to make their way to Turnip Rock, out at Point aux Barques. This will require paddling out on Lake Huron. It is a good idea to plan ahead for this one. Turnip Rock it is a beautiful formation which is also a tiny tidal island. It got it's name from it's distinctive. The likeness to a turnip is enhanced by the tall trees and vegetation growing on top of the rock's surface. This turnip shape of the rock is the result of thousands of years of waves and storms eroding the base away. The water around the rock are quite shallow, making it possible to get out, wade around a bit and take pictures. The lake bottom is rocky and slippery, proper footwear is essential.

About the only way to get there is on the water, all of the shoreline is private property. It is about 3.5 miles from Port Austin. Depending on the weather, that can take more than an hour following the recommended route along the shore line, so you aren't out on one of the Great Lakes out of sight of land. The shoreline can be used, but this is all private property. The homeowners appreciate it if paddlers don't set up camp.

Some visitors want to take in the lighthouse as well. That is a more difficult trip that is for experienced paddlers on the calmest of days. Regardless of which destination you are interested in, accurate information is necessary for a safe excursion. You can get all of that and advice on where to launch from Port Austin Kayak & Bike Rental.

They know these waters and can help visitors have fun. It may only be a couple miles out along the shoreline, but conditions on the Great Lakes can become difficult, or downright dangerous, very quickly.

TOP OF THE LAKE GETAWAY

There are cities and towns all along the 1,632 miles of Lake Michigan shoreline. Some have become big, famous, and crowded. Some, like Naubinway, at the "Top Of The Lake", are gateways to a different time and way of life. Naubinway is as far north as you can get on Lake Michigan, and is the largest commercial fishing port on the Great Lakes, in the Upper Peninsula. This is also the way to the Hiawatha National Forest with its miles of trails, rivers, streams and numerous lakes. Then, there are those beautiful uncrowded beaches, miles of them. The word Naubinway is an Indian word meaning "Places of Echoes". I can understand that. The entire area is surrounded by silent forests and natural beauty.

Getting there is an easy drive with a gorgeous scenic views. The stretch of U.S. Highway 2 from St. Ignace to the east, and Thompsonville near Manistique to the west, is a designated Scenic Byway. You don't even need to use the road. The marina at Naubinway is ready to welcome visitors arriving by boat. A getaway to the Top Of The Lake involves exploring northern Lake Michigan from Epoufette to Gould City with, perhaps, a foray or two into the Hiawatha National Forest. Right in the middle of it all is Naubinway, and the Top Of The Lake Region. Visitors will find unique local attractions, gorgeous nature areas, festivals, and those unique "yooper" eats.

There are trails of every kind all over the area. Beach trails here are especially beautiful. One stretch of sand, on Lake Michigan, is known as the "east beach" at Epoufette. Another is known as the "west beach" at Scott's Point. This part of the Lake Michigan shoreline has become a popular walking tour. If a long trek is not what you are after, you could just drive on over to Scott's Point. The beach is gorgeous. There are picnic areas and a pavilion. Of special note, the comfort facilities are rustic, but they are excellent. They include large cedar paneled changing rooms that are second to none. The beach also serves as a nature trail. All this is just a few miles south of Gould City. If you are looking for trails and wilderness, away from the big lake, the Seney Wildlife Refuge is just the place. There are 95,212 acres of wilderness, swamps, islands, and lakes. Visitors are liable to encounter trumpeter swans, osprey, loons, deer, turtles, geese, fish, eagles, and even the occasional moose!

In addition to the trails and wilderness areas, there are great inland fishing lakes. Lake Millecoquins, one of the largest, is a 1,062 acre lake with a maximum depth of about 12 feet. Fishermen go after the walleye, pike, perch, bluegill, and largemouth and smallmouth Bass. In fact, Lake Millecoquins has been rated one of the best Smallmouth Bass lakes in Michigan. This is also a favorite destination for ice fishing. There is access to the lake from a public ramp, off Indian Trail Road, and from within the Hiawatha Sportsman's Club. Lake

Millecoquins must have an interesting history, the name is French for "lake of a thousand rascals".

It isn't all wilderness and water, there is other fun to be found here. Members rave about the Hiawatha Sportsman's Club. I can tell you that visitors will enjoy it too, especially the excellent golf course found there. There is the fascinating Cut River Bridge, Garlyn Zoo, the Historical Museum in Engadine and the one-of-a-kind Snowmobile Museum. There are "yooper" shops around like the 906 Hunting Company and the Cut River store. That Snowmobile Museum has a big gift shop, as well.

One place has all the directions and information, head for that Top Of The Lake Snowmobile Museum, right in the middle of Naubinway. This is a case where the name of the place just can't tell the whole story. When you visit, you will find yourself in one of the most unique places in the entire upper peninsula. The museum has an incredible variety of snow machines on display. One of the highlights of the museum collection is the 1946 Eliason. This brand is said to be the first marketed snowmobile in the form that was the beginning of the product that we know of today. It was first built by Carl Eliason of Sayner, WI. in the back of his general store about 1920.

All this fun is going to make you hungry. People who only visit the upper peninsula occasionally, are often in search of two specialties of the region, smoked fish and pasties. If that is what you are looking for, a quick and easy getaway to the Top Of The Lake is just the ticket. Two of the businesses here get consistently top, 5 star reviews from locals and travelers alike. Hiawatha Pasties makes them from a traditional recipe. Some say they are the best in the eastern upper peninsula. Then there is Campfire BBQ in Gould City. While not a traditional BBQ, theirs is consistently voted as a "must try". In addition to smoked, you can get fresh fish right off the docks here. This is fish with a freshness measured in hours, not days. There are other dining options ranging from cozy dining to those specializing in serving up a hearty upper peninsula breakfast.

The "Top Of The Lake" is one of the best kept secrets in all of the upper peninsula. There is so much to do and enjoy that you may want to stay a while. Lodging options include rustic campgrounds, cabins, inns and B&B's.

WALLOON GETAWAY

Walloon Lake really is a quaint destination, the entire town is only a few city blocks long. Still, for a quick getaway there is plenty to do and you won't face the manic pace and crowds found at some of the more famous towns in Northern Michigan. The short list includes lakeside dining with awesome views, both trendy and upscale, a general store, bakery, shops, parks, hiking and snowmobile trails, and a luxury hotel. Much of what happens here centers around the lake. It is big enough, 4,000+ acres, to support every kind of water sport. The lake water is as clear as it was when Ernest Hemingway fished here a hundred years ago. The beach invites sun-bathers and swimmers. Walloon Lake is great for kayaks, paddle boards, boating and most any other lake activity. If you bring your own equipment you will find that the public boat launch is excellent. If you want to have fun on the lake, but don't want to haul equipment on a day trip, the local outfitter at the beach can provide everything from boards to pontoon boats of every description, to guided tours. Some visitors come just to play in the park and hang out on the beach.

The township park that is right across the road from the beach. This is where you find people playing Pickle Ball, a sport that combines elements of badminton, tennis, and table tennis. Players use solid paddles to hit a perforated polymer ball, similar to a wiffle ball, over a net. There is old-fashioned shuffle board, a beach swing, picnic areas and the river flows along one edge of the park. If you follow the river you will come to the trail access that is great for hiking in the warm months and snowshoeing in the winter. One reason that this park is so much fun is that, after a solid 15 minutes or so of healthy vigorous exercise, one can make it to an ice cream stand of a comfy spot for a cold one, just by walking half a block. Everything in Walloon Lake is close by and there is lots of parking.

Some people visit Walloon just for the festivals. The last weekend in April is when the village gets going with Hemingway Weekend. A major event, Celebrate Walloon, takes place in July. In the past, activities have included music, an art show from Walloon Art Club, face painting, rides on the lake courtesy of Walloon Sailors and a petting Zoo. The Conservancy has provided an educational presentation. They explain some of the species that are appearing in Michigan lakes and the impact they have. In August it is all about the antique boats. Walloon Woodies is a group of wooden boat owners who gather the first Saturday in August to parade their boats down Walloon Lake. These are those great old vintage boats. In past years there have been a couple of dozen in the parade.

You can't talk about outdoor fun in Northern Michigan without considering the great trails that are found here. The park has access to a couple of great ones. There is a hiking trail that follows the river. It is an easy walk in the warm months and a pretty good workout on snow shoes in the winter. The Petoskey Snowmobile Trail can also be accessed at the park. Just north of Walloon Lake, on Country Club Road is the Postle Farm Preserve with several cool trails. In a region where most nature preserves are kind of wild, this one preserves an historic agricultural environment. The Postle Farm Preserve consists of 113 acres, encompassing three distinct habitats. The habitats include, an open field farmstead area, a northern hardwood forest area and a low meadow wetland area. Each habitat can be explored via easy loop trails in a family friendly environment. The longest loop is only one mile long. The Postle Farm Preserve contains some of the first cross country ski trails ever developed in Northern Michigan. Long before the sport became a craze, these trails were created by a few enthusiasts from the Sierra Club. There is a rumor that this is where the elusive morel mushroom hides.

The village is small, so it is easy to get a little shopping in. There is a general store and Tommy's, the outfitter, where you can rent all manner of equipment. Unique to this area are the Pop Up Shops. These are small enclosed kiosks that are open seasonally with a range of gifts and Michigan items. All of the "pop ups" are located along a small alcove or alley. The shop that shouldn't be missed is Vintage Mercantile. It is an antiques, gift and home décor shop. Many of their items are unique to Northern Michigan, especially Walloon Lake's, historic past. The store has been nominated for best Antique and Vintage store in the Petoskey News Best of 2016 competition! The shop is located in an historic cabin and is filled top to bottom with antiques and vintage finds. Plan to spend some time inside, the variety of merchandise is amazing, and there is no space that isn't filled to capacity. Vintage Mercantile is located directly across the street from Hotel Walloon.

Dining venues of every kind are found here. Fine dining is available at a couple of spots. The Walloon Lake Inn has been here since the late 1800s and is regularly reviewed for its delicious selections. If you want to sit by the lake and have an eclectic dining adventure, the menu at the Barrel Back is for you. It is generally agreed that their smoked wings are the second best wings found in any Michigan restaurant. If you are looking for simpler fare or want supplies for a picnic, the deli at the Walloon Lake General Store is the place to go.

Walloon Lake is fun for a winter getaway as well. The ring of grass in the center of the park becomes a free ice skating rink. The Postle Farm Preserve contains some of the first cross country ski trails ever developed in Northern Michigan. The Petoskey Snowmobile Trail runs through the park. And yes, you can even rent snowshoes in town. Some say that the ice fishing here is second to none, especially for trout.

There is something else rare and wonderful here. There is a trail along the lake shore that Hemingway used back when he would come here. The trail is not a formal trail and is not marked. You just need to know where it is. What you do is make your way to the flagpole at the Walloon Lake Inn. That is where the trail starts. It follows the shoreline of the lake for about a mile. This is an informal trail that is actually crossing private property. The property owners don't mind, but appreciate being respected while you walk the path that Ernest Hemingway walked a century ago. This is Ernest Hemingway country. The area inspired two books, "Up In Michigan" and "Big Two-Hearted River". There is an historical marker across from the Walloon Lake beach that tells some of the story. The cottage of Windemere is still here on the lake, though it is not open to the public. Walloon Lake is off Highway 131, halfway between Boyne Falls and Petoskey.

MONTAGUE

IS

AT

ONE

END

OF

THE

HART

MONTAGUE

TRAIL

WHITE LAKE GETAWAY

It might seem odd to plan a getaway to a lake that is very nearly a part of Lake Michigan, but White Lake is so charming that many people do just that. White Lake is connected to Lake Michigan by the White River. In addition to an the natural beauty of the lakes, streams, overlooks and trails, the White Lake area offers the visitor the arts, unique shops, historic lighthouses, and great festivals. In every season, the principal towns of Montague and Whitehall, welcome visitors to shop, dine and relax for a day.

The shopping venues in both towns include antiques, boutiques, and art galleries. The Book Nook is a favorite in day time. Their entertainment includes space to browse the books, gourmet coffees and cakes, and regular live music performances. In the evening, some people travel here for live theatre. The Howmet Playhouse offers an intimate 400-seat venue for lyric and musical theatre, jazz, blues, folk and classical concerts, screen presentations, fundraisers and business meetings. This theatre is unique in several ways. It is one of only a handful of theatres that was constructed with a plaster "Kappeldome". This feature, named after a German designer, enhances the acoustics and ensures that voices are projected throughout the theatre. The acoustics at the Howmet Playhouse are among the best in Western Michigan.

Historic attractions are close by as well, you can't miss the World's Tallest Weather Vane. Standing nearly 50 feet tall, it is right down by the waterfront. On the top of the weather vane is a ship that depicts the 157 ton lumber schooner, Ella Ellenwood. The White River Lighthouse, built in 1875 by Captain William Robinson, is just south of town. The White River Light Station is now a museum. Visitors can climb the spiral staircase to the top of the lighthouse tower and peruse the 19th and early 20th century photographs. There is an excellent collection of nautical artifacts and a stunning view across Lake Michigan.

Other visitors come for the natural beauty. White Lake and the White River are part of the lifestyle. Swans are abundant on the lake. Boating, sailing and fishing are favorite past-times including ice fishing events in winter. The Hart/Montague Trail provides opportunities for hiking, biking and bird watching. The trail is a State Park and is a paved 22-mile linear trail converted from an old railroad corridor. It opened in 1991 providing passage through rural, forested areas with scenic overlooks and picnic areas along the way. The trail bridge, over the White River, is just the beginning of a great day of nature site seeing. Travelers along the trail will find meadows, orchards, fields and even a section of old Michigan prairie. Bird watchers will be rewarded with a huge variety of species and I encourage you to take a camera along. Hikers may see a wide diversity of wildlife and spot a variety of songbirds year round.

There is something else rare and wonderful here, remnants of the Schooner Ellenwood. The 157 ton lumber schooner, Ella Ellenwood, was built in Saginaw, Michigan and was operated out of White Lake, by Captain Thomas Flagstad. On the night of October 1, 1901, while bound for Milwaukee, Wisconsin with a load of maple edgings and shingles, the Ella Ellenwood ran aground off Fox Point, about 8 miles from the Milwaukee harbor. Within hours the northerly winds and waves began to break the proud vessel apart. The captain and crew were compelled to abandon ship. By the next day the ship's fate was sealed and she was soon gone; her cargo lost. The following spring, a portion of the wooden nameplate "ELLENWOOD", was found inside White Lake channel. Somehow, the nameplate had drifted across Lake Michigan and found its way into the narrow channel leading to White Lake. She had found her way home. That nameplate, over 100 years old, and a scale model of the Ellenwood are exhibited in the downstairs lobby of the Montague City Hall.

NOTES

NOTES

NOTES

NOTES

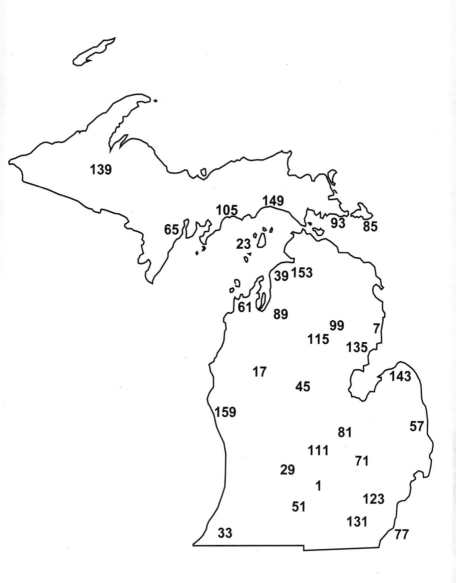